HARRIET QUIMBY
Flying Fair Lady

LESLIE KERR

4880 Lower Valley Road • Atglen, PA 19310

Other Schiffer Books on Related Subjects:

17 Women Who Shook the World, Preethi Burkholder, 978-0-7643-4141-0

Courageous Women of Maryland, Katharine Kenny and Eleanor Randrup, 978-0-7643-3541-9

Chesapeake Women: Their Stories, Their Memories, Don Parks, 978-0-7643-4701-6

Designed by Molly Shields
Cover design by Brenda McCallum
Type set in Adorn Copperplate/Adobe Caslon Pro

Credits and disclaimer: Photos and illustrations credited unless source unknown. Every effort has been made in this regard.

ISBN: 978-0-7643-5067-2
Printed in China

Published by Schiffer Publishing, Ltd.
4880 Lower Valley Road
Atglen, PA 19310
Phone: (610) 593-1777; Fax: (610) 593-2002
E-mail: Info@schifferbooks.com

For our complete selection of fine books on this and related subjects, please visit our website at www.schifferbooks.com. You may also write for a free catalog.

This book may be purchased from the publisher. Please try your bookstore first.

We are always looking for people to write books on new and related subjects. If you have an idea for a book, please contact us at proposals@schifferbooks.com.

DEDICATION

To Grant, who has made life a joy, and to Drew, my inspiration.

Contents

Acknowledgments

It was the stunning, plum-hued flying outfit the mannequin wore that first caught my eye. My husband and I were touring the Cradle of Aviation Museum in Garden City, New York, with our friends, Alan and "Sam" Cagan. Amelia Earhart came to mind, but Alan, a pilot and a docent at the museum, informed me that, in fact, the lady before us was Miss Harriet Quimby. After learning something of her remarkable life that day, the journalist in me was curious to know more. Alan has continued to be a vital resource throughout the development of her story.

Melissa Keiser of the Smithsonian Institution Air & Space Museum Research Library was most generous with her time, as were the staff members at the Museum of Modern Art (MoMA) in New York City; the Arroyo Grande Library in San Luis Obispo County, California; the Academy of Motion Picture Arts and Sciences in Los Angeles; and the Library of Congress Digital Collections in Washington, DC.

My daughter-in-law, Diana Palcic, was instrumental in helping me with technical challenges a project like this entails. My editors at Schiffer Publishing, Bob Biondi and Cheryl Weber, were most supportive and helped to reinforce my belief in the scope of Harriet's message.

My love and appreciation go to Drew, my unofficial reviewer, and to Grant, both of whom understand what this story represents to me.

Last, but certainly not least, a very special thanks goes to Miss Harriet Quimby. Thank goodness we have the 250-plus stories she wrote throughout the course of her life that offer insight into all she stood for. Her legacy touches us all.

INTRODUCTION

"A chafing dish, a tea caddy, and a genial friend who understands you and is glad over your little successes and silent over your failures, goes a long way toward real contentment."
—Harriet Quimby

Did she really believe this sentiment? This lady, who challenged the Victorian mores in which she lived her brief thirty-seven years, who through 250 or more articles filed during her journalism career championed equality for women and minorities and served as the mouthpiece for many social injustices we still face today? This lady of many "firsts": the first female journalist to use a typewriter and the first to use a camera to capture photos that would enhance her stories; the first female in the US to receive a driver's license and to purchase her own automobile; the first woman in the US to earn her pilot's license; the first American female to fly across the English Channel; the first woman to design flight attire for female pilots; the first female brand spokesperson for an American advertising campaign. Who knows what other firsts this extraordinary lady might have achieved had she lived.

Any one of these achievements posed a threat to the Victorian male in an era when women knew their place, but together these accomplishments were impossible for most men to comprehend. Still, though never a proclaimed feminist—quite the opposite— Harriet Quimby did assert her right to live life to the fullest and encouraged others to do the same, and her beauty, charm, and sense of adventure brought her much admiration and respect from all she met throughout her personal and professional life.

It is surprising that more has not been written about this phenomenal woman so ahead of her time. Amelia Earhart talked of Quimby's accomplishments in aviation and her admiration for the person who paved the way for women in flight, but there is so much more to Harriet Quimby. Recognition for the far-reaching contributions of this flying fair lady is long overdue.

Chapter One

MICHIGAN FARM GIRL (1875–1888)

"All lives are molded, more or less, by our first teachings. True courtesy, sympathy, and sincerity are the most powerful factors for good in either home or public life."
—Harriet Quimby

Branch County is in southern Michigan, halfway between Chicago and Detroit along the old Sauk Trail, a former Indian path now more commonly known as US 12 Heritage Route. Nineteen miles from the Indiana border, Branch is considered one of ten Michigan "cabinet counties" named after President Andrew Jackson and members of his cabinet. Branch County honored the seventh president's first Navy secretary John Branch.

Coldwater is the largest of four quaint communities within Branch County and according to some reports it was here, on May 11, 1875, that Harriet Quimby was born to William Quimby and the former Ursula Cook. Although Harriet's birth certificate has never been found, Michiganders from Coldwater, as well as numerous townships throughout the state, have since claimed her as their native child.

William Quimby, one of six children, was the son of Irish immigrants. Not much is known about his education, but he grew up on a farm in upstate New York. Ursula, too, spent her childhood in New York, the daughter of a well-educated family. Her father, known as A. Cook, was considered a renowned chemist and her brother Joseph was a successful New York physician. Ursula's family practiced what were said to be progressive medical beliefs. A. Cook had concocted a remedy he called Cook's Liver Invigorator and Blood Purifier, which he promoted as a perfect cleanser for any ailment of the blood, kidneys, liver, heart, stomach, or spine. It could, he professed, also help with bilious liver, fever, jaundice, rheumatism, and even female weakness—a true wonder potion. The recipe for this tonic served as the base for Ursula's own concoction of native herbs when the family relocated to Michigan some years later.

William met Ursula when he returned to New York after his discharge from the Union Army. A limp sustained from a childhood injury kept him from the front lines, so William begrudgingly served as regimental cook with B Company of the 188th Regiment New York Infantry until severe dysentery required his early discharge. He never experienced what some Civil War historians called "bitter action." Although his regiment was at Appomattox when Lee surrendered to Grant in 1865, William was too ill to participate in the victory ceremonies. He was, however, one of the few survivors of the entire 188th Regimental—almost all had succumbed to dysentery before the war's end. William's service provided him with a $12-a-month pension for the remainder of his life. This and the promise of a bright future motivated William and Ursula to leave New York for Michigan. It is unclear why the couple chose Michigan, but records indicate that other Quimby and Cook relatives had previously relocated to Coldwater.

Marriage records in Branch County, Coldwater, Michigan, show that the couple wed on October 9, 1859. Although seemingly mismatched from the start, they were united in their resolve to better their lives, wherever that might lead. William worked their small rock farm, while Ursula concocted and peddled the family elixir to locals to supplement their meager income. Nine Quimby children were born before Harriet came along in 1875, but only she and her sister Helen, known as Kittie, born in 1870, survived.

Harriet inherited the milky white complexion, deep-set blue eyes, and long, lean elegance of her father and the silky, blue-black hair of her mother. Unlike William, whose constitution was never strong, Ursula remained young-looking long after the rest of her body gave way to the strain of years of moving and farm labor. Her personality was a dominant family influence. Harriet spent her formative years molded by Ursula's convictions regarding women's emancipation. She firmly believed women should not have to depend on a man for happiness and success. Ursula was determined that neither of her girls would perform the backbreaking, not to mention aging, work required of farmers. Harriet learned her lessons well. Kittie, however, eloped at age fourteen shortly after the family moved to California in 1884 and was never heard from again. In correspondence or conversation thereafter, Harriet never mentioned her only sibling.

The rock farm did not do well, and by the time Harriet was five, the family had picked up stakes again. The 1880 census found them in the small town of Arcadia, Manistee County, in the far northwest corner of the state, where William once again tried his hand at farming on the banks of Lake Michigan. It takes time for a new farm to succeed, so he worked part-time for local lumber companies to support his family.

During these early years, Harriet's environment consisted of neighbors dependent upon neighbors, strong religious beliefs, and a community united through the local church and school. Harriet attended grammar school a few miles away and by all accounts did well. Before long, Manistee boasted a large grocery store and several small, thriving businesses, in addition to the major sources of industry—logging and fishing.

Things were going well for the Quimbys in the mid-1880s, until for reasons unknown, the family let the farm settle into receivership. Most likely, its demise was a result of impending disastrous times for the country. In desperation, William tried his hand at running the town's general store, but with no business acumen he failed miserably. Undaunted, Ursula took control of her family's fate once again, and by doing so, re-charted Harriet's destiny. She convinced her husband to move west to California. Jobs there were more plentiful and the economy more stable, she reasoned. So William, ever wanting to please his wife, agreed. It would be yet another new start for the Quimbys.

This time the family journeyed halfway across the country, to Arroyo Grande, California, a small farming community tucked between Los Angeles and San Francisco. The trek was not easy. The Quimbys gathered their minimal belongings and backtracked across Michigan to Lansing, where they caught the train for Chicago. From there they boarded the Union Pacific Railroad for San Francisco.

The weary travelers took a stagecoach for the long, dusty trip to Arroyo Grande. No one knows why William and Ursula, now in their mid-sixties, chose Arroyo Grande, except that farming was what they knew and there was farmland by the acre to be had in the early years of California's statehood. Land records in 1885 report the family owning a small farm. Even today, this central region of the Golden State boasts rich farmland and open spaces. A change in location, however, did not improve William's luck as a farmer. This venture, too, failed and he was forced to take a job at a large dairy farm. As the 1890s began, life for Harriet and her family looked grim—to all but Ursula.

For the country overall, the 1890s brought unstable times. The Panic of 1893, the worst economic depression the nation had experienced at that time, occurred during the Gilded Age in the midst of unprecedented economic expansion. However, this prosperity, driven by railroad speculation, spurred over-building and out-of-control spending, leading to bank failures and financial disaster across the country. Silver glutted the market and its price crashed. Farmers in the heartland struggled under a decline in prices for agricultural commodities. When the Philadelphia and Reading Railroad went bankrupt in February 1883, panic ensued. People flocked to withdraw their money, and the bank runs and credit crunch rippled through the economy. Stock prices dropped, 500 banks shuttered their doors, 15,000 business failed, and farms across the nation ceased operations. Desperate citizens chopped wood, broke rocks, and in some cases turned to prostitution to feed their families. Unemployment soared. In states like Michigan, which the Quimbys had called home, unemployment reached a staggering forty-three percent.

Ursula persuaded her husband it was time to move again—to San Francisco. The city was where they needed to be to seek their fortune, she was certain. In fact, Ursula had long ago decided she wanted more—if not for herself, then for Harriet. Once again, William had no rebuttal. The family gathered all they had left and headed north.

Once settled in San Francisco, life appeared to improve for the Quimbys. California schools in the latter part of the nineteenth century offered a solid education from grammar school through college. Liberal and unrestricted by New England puritanical attitudes, California women owned property, ran businesses, and held administrative positions in companies and civic organizations. William became an itinerant salesman, peddling from the back of a wagon what had now become Quimby's Liver Invigorator. Ursula augmented their still-meager income by making prune sacks for the local fruit packing industry. Still, she was thrilled and well on her way to grooming Harriet for the life she had longed for herself.

This more sophisticated city environment allowed Ursula to build the persona of a young woman who would not only boast "eastern blood lines," but who was as talented as she was beautiful. Through her relentless image-building campaign, Ursula nurtured Harriet's self-confidence and taste for attention. She shaved nine years from her daughter's age and told friends Harriet had been born in Boston and educated in Switzerland and France. Harriet graduated from Los Gatos High School in 1897, along with other ambitious young women who wanted to attend college and enter professions like teaching, medicine, or law. Ursula wanted Harriet to pursue a career in journalism. This, she told her daughter, was a respectable profession, but more important, one where she could attain prominence and meet the right people. Harriet had other aspirations. She wanted to be an actress.

Chapter Two

COMING OF AGE IN CALIFORNIA (1888–1903)

"Something tells me that I shall do something someday."
—Harriet Quimby

In 1900, Harriet was twenty-five years old (sixteen if you asked her mother). That year's census reported her living with her parents at 420 Montgomery Street, close to Chinatown amid the artists, writers, and actors who gathered at the Bohemian Club. The Montgomery Street residence was described as a "hovel" where Harriet slept on the couch and whose walls were layered with head shots of Harriet, by then working as a model.

How Harriet's talents as an actress developed is unknown. There is no record of any formal training. Friends described her as "vivacious, ambitious, alive, and charming, with a low, resonate voice, brilliant smile, and an innate sense of style" (*San Francisco Call*, 1903). Others commented that her only flaw, barely perceptible in photos, was a slightly chipped front tooth. These attributes were not her mother's creation. Harriet recognized her strengths and used her charms however and whenever she chose to reinvent herself throughout her life.

At the dawn of the twentieth century, an "actress" in polite circles meant "a beautiful bobble on the arm of men who could afford her…" (Philip, 1991). Still, Harriet did perform in local theater productions. William, always eager to appease his wife, now traveled as far away as Oregon to peddle Ursula's liver concoction.

Harriet became the main support for her family by clerking in a mercantile shop by day and moonlighting as an extra at the Clay Clement Company's Columbia Theater most nights. It was here that she became friends with D. W. Griffith and his soon-to-be wife Linda Arvidson, struggling thespians in long-since-forgotten San Francisco theaters. The trio also honed their craft at the Olympia and Alcazar Theaters. Harriet and Linda bartered with photographer Arnold Genthe for promotional pictures and borrowed $40 from San Francisco Mayor James Phalen to rent the Alcazar theater hall for a lavish production of *Romeo and Juliet*. Early in her brief theatrical career, Harriet went by the stage name Hazel Quimby. In this production, she played Romeo. Linda, using the name Lina Johnson, portrayed Juliet. Thanks to her friend Charlotte Thompson, who covered their performances for the *San Francisco Dramatic Review*, Harriet next landed a small role in *Sapho* starring Florence Roberts, a popular actress of the day. Griffith had not yet found his niche as the controversial director for Biograph Pictures. He and Linda married in 1907, and she would star in many of her husband's films throughout her life.

Many stage door Johnnies vied for Harriet's attention. However, other than a rumored affair with Griffith, whose reputation as a ladies' man followed him all the way to Hollywood, Harriet was never officially linked to any one gentleman. This was fine with Ursula, who had come to resent her own marriage and was determined her daughter would not follow the same path. Though Harriet's theatrical career proved short-lived, she would rekindle her friendship with the Griffiths a few years later on the East Coast, when Harriet's journalism career was well-established. In fact, Harriet is credited with writing seven screenplays for Griffith at Biograph, making her the first recorded female scriptwriter in the nation—one of many firsts Harriet would claim in her brief lifetime.

Beautiful and intelligent, and with an eye for detail, Harriet loved to explore the nooks and crannies of Chinatown and the Wharf with her bohemian friends. This was an era of experimentation in the arts by people such as Isadora Duncan and Enrico Caruso, who performed in exotic places around the world. Harriet wanted to experience it all.

Her photographer friend Arnold Genthe probably introduced Harriet to the camera during this time. Born in Berlin and trained as a philosopher, Genthe emigrated to San Francisco in 1895 to work as a tutor and taught himself photography instead. So popular were his photographs that he opened his own portrait studio and rubbed elbows with Jack London, Nora Mae French, and Sarah Bernhardt. He was known as a Svengali, coaxing women of all social strata into posing for his camera. Genthe is responsible for the only remnant of Harriet's acting career: a nude photo of her that hung above the bar in the infamous Bohemian Club until the landmark was destroyed in the 1906 earthquake.

The Bohemian Club, founded in 1872, was by 1906 a regular gathering place for artists, musicians, and journalists. Newspaper writers were synonymous with the Bohemian identity, and writers such as Bret Harte and Mark Twain considered themselves bohemian. When the club rose from the rubble after the quake, it re-emerged as a prominent private establishment with members that included presidents, CEOs, captains of industry, and media moguls. It was the perfect setting for Harriet to explore her journalistic aspirations.

Harriet's first articles written for the *San Francisco Chronicle* and *San Francisco Call* were inspired by her association with Genthe and other Bohemian Club friends including Ambrose Bierce, Jack London, George Sterling, and Joaquin Miller, as well as *Call* editor Will Irwin. Famous for bawdy gatherings in Carmel and Monterey, the friends danced naked in the woods, feasted with wine, and thrived on the freedom of artistry. Serious literature emerged from Sterling, Miller, and others who became famous for capturing the beauty of California's rugged coast.

Harriet's first piece for the *Call* (c. 1901) was a front page Sunday supplement feature entitled "The Artists' Colony at Monterey." It captured her experience of this eclectic coastal existence.

> Monterey, from the fisher folk by the sea to the heart of the forest—adobes, sand dunes, cypress, oaks, pine, sea or wood and color, nowhere will one find the iridescent flights, now purple, now gray, that gleam through the mists in the soft tope so wonderfully beautiful as are found here in this region of solemnity and peace, coupled with its exceptional historic interest . . .

Another early contribution to the *Chronicle* appeared in the February 2, 1902 article entitled "A Night at a Haunted House." This turned out to be a rare work of fiction, as Harriet much preferred nonfiction. She told friends she would one day try her hand at novel-writing, but at that point in her life, it didn't pay the bills. In fact, Harriet's real talent was to transform an ordinary story into an armchair adventure for her readers. As she explored the streets of San Francisco, she was fascinated with the city's sounds, smells, and sights, and brought these scenes to life. *Call* editor Will Irwin, who published Harriet's first writing, described Harriet as having the keenest nose for news he had ever met in a woman. Her work touched the rawness of the human condition in exposé pieces like "How White Slaves are Shackled: The Astounding Disclosures of a Secret Investigation" that exposed the issue of prostitution in the US and allegedly led to a local police commissioner's downfall. Harriet would probe many such provocative issues in her writing.

Chinatown proved an inexhaustible source of material. One of her pieces, published in the *Overland Chronicle* and entitled "The Sacred Furnace of Mon War," described the ancient Chinese religious practice of burning paper documents. The residents of San Francisco's Chinatown reinterpreted this tradition by ceremoniously disposing of paper in the Pacific Ocean so that it might be returned to the shores of China. Accompanying the story were several photographs, perhaps taken by her confidant Arnold Genthe, but they might have been Harriet's own. She was becoming proficient with the camera.

Harriet's friends often reported that she was never more at home than when out and about—referring to her voracious love for travel and adventure. The passion with which Harriet described her existence reflects a young woman inspired by her surroundings at the moment and her exposure to many exciting men and women. Still, Harriet kept her professional and private lives separate. Only in the early days in Monterey was a serious romance ever rumored. Several years after her death, Harriet's friend Clara Bell Brown alluded to an unrequited romance with an unnamed Latin artist from which Harriet never recovered. Only two who frequented the Monterey artists' hangouts during that period in Harriet's life were possible candidates. Ernesto Peixotto and Xavier Martinez could have vied for Harriet's attention; Martinez was one of the Bohemian Club regulars when Harriet frequented the club.

Possibly Harriet understood that any type of relationship or hint of marriage would have prohibited the life and career she planned for herself. Though very much influenced by her mother's convictions regarding women's emancipation from a stifling Victorian lifestyle, Harriet adamantly claimed she was not a feminist. She believed adversarial tactics were inflammatory and impeded women's progress. Harriet did support a woman's right to vote, but more importantly advocated that anyone, male or female, should have the opportunity to experience life to the fullest.

As her reputation as a writer expanded, so did the topics she addressed. Soon she became known for her intelligent, descriptive, detailed reporting on a variety of subjects. Doors that would otherwise not be open to any reporter, let alone a female, seemed to open for her. Even though many narrow-minded editors were reluctant to take a female reporter seriously, Harriet was undeterred. No one was more pleased than her mother when Harriet announced her move to New York to make her mark as a journalist.

Chapter Three

THE BELLE OF NEW YORK (1903–1910)

"Always be well-gloved and well-shod and the dress will take care of itself. 'It is very simple,' advises the woman who has never earned a slice of bread and butter in her life and would probably starve if she were suddenly left to support herself."
—Harriet Quimby

Harriet arrived at Pennsylvania Station on a bleak January morning in 1903. It intimidated her with its immense glass ceiling and towering steel columns rising from track level to well over 100 feet. Strands of sunlight tinted with billowing clouds of smoke permeated the tunnels as she climbed the stairs to the main terminal. The great clock above the station's entrance read five minutes past noon. The whole scene fascinated her. She wondered when electricity had replaced coal-burning engines and if the seven-bulb chandeliers that hung from the gargantuan 200-foot ceiling really provided enough light at night. The white marble stairs she had climbed and six massive white marble Corinthian columns lining each side of the vaulted hall reminded her of a vision of ancient Rome in its finest hour. She glanced around. The terminal was crowded with people pushing every which way looking for friends, relatives, or perhaps other trains.

For a brief moment, she was overwhelmed. She realized she knew no one in New York City, had no place to live, and did not know where to look for a job. Harriet had always understood the value of not burning bridges and had made sure to negotiate a standing offer from Will Irwin in San Francisco to return to work at the *Call* any time. She also knew that New York City had pockets of crime and risky neighborhoods where an unescorted woman was a potential target. She was warned before leaving San Francisco not to venture downtown alone to look for a place to live. Irwin had also provided Harriet with the name of a woman who owned a boarding house on the Upper East

Side, so she ignored the bulletin board just inside the station advertising boarding houses and apartments to let. She would contact Irwin's friend first thing in the morning.

With the help of a red cap, Harriet gathered her two steamer trunks and ventured forth to the streets of New York and the Pennsylvania Hotel. Almost immediately, men approached her to offer carriage service. She declined politely and followed the porter through horse droppings and puddles of dirty ice across the cobblestone street and into the grand hotel. In the lobby she absorbed every sound, sight, and smell: the elevator's shiny brass and copper motif, the rich mahogany wood walls and exquisite paintings adorning the hallways, elderly gentlemen seated in velvet armchairs smoking cigars and reading newspapers or absorbed in chess. She wondered who they were—Vanderbilts or Morgans, perhaps? Harriet smiled to herself. New York was the kind of challenge she relished.

It wasn't until she locked the door to the bath closet down the hall from her room that she allowed herself to breathe a sigh of relief. Five days on the sooty train had left her body badly in need of soap and water. She did not like the idea of bathing in a shared hotel bath. But anything was welcome at the moment.

She lay back in the tub and reflected on her experience thus far. The implication of the hotel clerk's remarks as he glanced at her luggage suddenly dawned on her. "You're only staying one night?" he had asked rather skeptically, she thought. When she showed the clerk a letter of introduction from Will Irwin stating her profession as journalist, his demeanor had softened. Now Harriet realized that he had assumed the worst of a woman traveling alone in New York. So this was New York City, she thought. A whole new world awaited her.

Early the next morning, Harriet contacted the boarding house owner and accepted the accommodations at Third Avenue and 68th Street on the Upper East Side. The rent, including three meals a day, was $3.50 a week. Rather pricey for the time, considering eggs cost fourteen cents a dozen and a man's suit sold for $10. The building did boast one newfangled notion: indoor plumbing, which Harriet certainly appreciated. Her neighbors were hardworking Irish and German immigrants seeking to build a better life in America. This charming young woman's warm demeanor and outgoing personality endeared her to the other boarders within a few days of her arrival.

Her next challenge was to find work. There were few women journalists in 1903, but those of any prominence were found on the East Coast. She knew most editors were skeptical of female reporters, even though women had been involved in the profession for over 150 years. Although doubt crept in as to whether her move East had been the right decision, Harriet resolved to withhold judgment until she got to know the town better. With her usual take-charge attitude, Harriet was determined to make her way. She began the rounds of newspaper offices.

In that era, publishing houses were clustered around downtown city hall in a section referred to as printing press row. Braving the rush hour crowds was a challenge. Harriet was used to the open-air trolleys of San Francisco, not the stifling Third Avenue trolley, where people squeezed together like cattle on the way to market. Nor was she used to the narrow streets, dirty from strewn garbage, horse-drawn carriages, and leftover slush from harsh winter snows. Her long skirt became soggy and soiled as she trudged along with the masses.

Harriet had brought along some of her previously published work and a few articles completed during her weeklong journey cross-country. She hoped these would sell and provide much-needed income until she landed a full-time job. She was savvy enough to know that in the final analysis she would be judged on what she could produce from her pen to make money for the publication that employed her, not for what she had accomplished in the past. Still, she hoped these writings would get her in the door.

Her first stop was *Leslie's Illustrated Newspaper* (later renamed *Leslie's Illustrated Weekly*). Founded in 1852, the paper was one of several international, magazine-style publications started by editor and illustrator Frank Leslie and known for its far-reaching illustrations and reports. Throughout its decades of existence, the *Weekly* provided stories and pictures from around the world—first with wood engravings and daguerreotypes, later with more advanced forms of photography. When covering controversies like John Brown's raid at Harpers Ferry, the Civil War, the Spanish-American War, and World War I, the paper often took a strongly patriotic stance. However, its articles also presented a wide variety of literary and informative topics—perfect for Harriet's broad range of interests and diverse writing talent. Among those writing for the *Weekly* were Louisa May Alcott, H. Irving Hancock, and Ellis Parker Butler. Several notable illustrators worked for the publication over the years, including Albert Berghaus and Norman Rockwell.

Harriet made a distinct first impression. The first assistant editor she encountered at *Leslie's* was impressed with her published clips but was not in a position to hire her. He introduced her to another associate who, though equally impressed, told her she would have to come back the next day to meet the editor-in-chief. Reluctantly, Harriet departed, returning the next morning promptly at 7:45. This time, the editor was there and invited her into his office.

She refused the cup of coffee he offered for fear that her trembling hands might destroy her chances. Nerves were not usual for her, but even Harriet knew this would be a turning point for her career. The editor, probably the *Weekly's* first and long-time chief, John Y. Foster, read her work and peered over his horn-rimmed glasses. "I would have said it this way," he began, and proceeded to recite his edited version of the entire work. When he finished, he glanced again at Harriet, who sat stone-faced. "See what I mean?"

She nodded graciously, but inside Harriet seethed. She was used to praise and, after all, hadn't she published and been paid for the piece he had just made his own? For now, she decided discretion was the better part of valor and simply smiled sweetly. Perhaps it was because she was a female or he was testing her ability to remain cool and collected, or perhaps he was captivated by Harriet. Whatever the reason, before she had a chance to speak, Foster changed his tone. He announced that he would take a chance on her. She could cover a few assignments for the paper initially and they would see how it went. This was fine with Harriet; she was prepared to accept any offer he might present.

Her enthusiasm was short-lived, for just as quickly, Foster switched gears again, asking Harriet why she would not want to consider another line of work—cooking or cleaning, perhaps? Another test, thought Harriet. She quickly quelled Foster's argument, stating that she had tried cooking and was certain the she could write better than she could cook. "Believe me, we will get along fine," she assured him. Harriet looked him directly in the eyes and a friendship began that would last the rest of Harriet's life (Holden, 1993).

This captivating beauty had ventured east with a different perspective on a woman's place in society, influenced by her mother and the more liberated life of women in the West. Yet universal suffrage was still decades away. While women in Wyoming had won the right to vote in state elections in 1869, men like George Bernard Shaw lamented, "You give women the right to vote and before long there will be a crushing tax on bachelors."

Foster had taken a chance on Harriet. Her first article, "Curious Chinese Customs," appeared on January 22, 1903, just three weeks after her arrival in New York. It was a fitting first venture, considering her deep curiosity about America's melting-pot culture and the social issues the nation faced. Harriet soon convinced the editors at *Leslie's* that she could cover many types of stories. She was on her way!

Her first assignments for *Leslie's* ranged from stories about the home and household to feature stories about New York's tenement lifestyles, social issues, and restaurant reviews. Her passion for the theater grew. She lost no time reaching out to theatrical friends—actors, theater managers, directors, and producers—who had also ventured east to seek their fortunes. Harriet asked to add theater reviews to her assignments and readers soon relied on her weekly column for entertaining accounts of Broadway happenings. *Leslie's* entertainment editor John Sleicher made Harriet the paper's drama critic, promoting her as "the most entertaining writer in the theatrical world" (*Leslie's Illustrated Weekly*, 1910). He boasted that anyone interested in "stage land topics" would learn much from Harriet's reviews and the trademark list of "Plays to Which One Can Take His Wife or Daughters" that she dutifully included at the end of each column.

Harriet's review of *The Chorus Lady* in 1906 typified her easy access to the theater community. Leading lady Rose Stahl, who played the title role in the hit comedy *Patricia*, granted Harriet a rare interview. The two had been friends in San Francisco and Stahl agreed to a "no perfume, no poodle, no parrots, no maid" thirty-minute exchange, which Harriet said had kept her laughing for the duration. In her story she quoted Patricia's favorite expression "smilin's the hard part of dancin'," which Stahl later added to her signature when autographing photos for fans (*Leslie's Illustrated Weekly*, 1906).

Though often generous with praise, Harriet was just as quick to barb that which she found distasteful. At the top of this list were noisy audiences, bad acting, and every now and again the hapless starlet whose fame Harriet would denounce as "not always deserving" (*Leslie's Illustrated Weekly*, 1906). Even so, readers sensed that her severest criticisms were based on thoughtful observation.

"Sermons may teach us how to die, but plays teach us how to live.
So much for the play's ethical value." —*Harriet Quimby*

With her reputation as a respected journalist growing, Harriet was determined to move to more spacious housing. She had quickly discovered the drawbacks of boarding house living. Quarters were cramped. People constantly moved in and out, trampling mud through the halls. Even worse, the constant parade of rodents and cockroaches sickened her. Between her theater reviews and other freelance assignments, within six months of arrival in New York Harriet was earning enough money to move to the Hotel Victoria on Twenty-seventh Street and Broadway. The eight-story building boasted the "latest plunger-type hydraulic elevator" reported to be the best and safest in the world (Holden, 1993). The rent was $1.50 per week. Charlotte Thompson, Harriet's colleague in San Francisco, had moved to New York after selling her short-lived *San Francisco Dramatic Review* and joined her friend at the Hotel Victoria. She quickly gained entré as a writer and her play *Helena Richie* received a glowing review from her old friend.

Life was exhilarating during this carefree time. The city's German and Irish immigrant population, the tenements of Delancy Street, and, of course, Chinatown, were a journalist's gold mine. By 1906, not only was Harriet an important part of *Leslie's* editorial staff, she contributed to many other newspapers and magazines throughout the city. She may have used pen names so as not to undermine her relationship with *Leslie's,* but this, or how many aliases she may have used, has never been confirmed.

What is known is that Harriet loved to travel, and as a self-proclaimed liberated woman, she often traveled unescorted. She filed at least a dozen articles from Cuba for *Leslie's,* which earned her another promotion. Harriet became *Leslie's Illustrated Weekly*'s first travel correspondent. Her prowess with the camera, learned from her friend Genthe, helped her land assignments in exotic places throughout Europe, Egypt, South America, and Africa. Images never seen before in the US titillated readers and enriched the descriptive stories she filed for her audiences. Although Harriet's journalism credits have been quoted frequently, her prolific, artistic photography was never fully acknowledged or appreciated until some time later, when dozens of her photos for *Leslie's Illustrated Weekly* travel articles were reproduced in a series of books entitled *Around the World with a Camera 1910–1919,* published by the Leslie-Judge Company.

About this time, the advent of the automobile provided Harriet with more of the exhilaration and freedom she craved. In the early twentieth century, the horse and carriage were a mark of elegance and social status. The automobile, thanks to Henry Ford and his Model T, was about to present a new opportunity for middle-class America to experience the freedom of the open road. As far back as 1821, Thomas Blanchard in Springfield, Massachusetts, had pioneered the assembly line concept of mass production and the use of interchangeable parts. In 1902, business tycoon Ransom Olds introduced large-scale production-line manufacturing at his Oldsmobile factory in Lansing,

Michigan. However, it was Henry Ford, expanding on Blanchard's processes, who made cars affordable to working-class Americans.

Automobiles were not new to Harriet. On assignment for *Leslie's* in 1906, she covered an auto race on Long Island. Enthralled, she used her charms to cajole a reluctant driver to take her "just once around the track" in his speed racer. She clutched her bonnet as they circled the track at 60–100 miles per hour. Her heart raced, she wrote later, and this first taste of danger associated with speed took her breath away. She penned the article "A Woman's Exciting Ride in a Motor Car," but that was not the end of it. Harriet was determined to take the next step.

Ford's Tin Lizzy rolled off the assembly line at the Henry Ford Motor Company on October 1, 1908, and into the hearts of the public. Shortly thereafter, Harriet managed to persuade someone to give her driving lessons; within a few weeks she obtained a driver's license, bought a car, and hit the road as the first woman in the US to not only receive her license, but to own an automobile.

During the next three years, women's access to cars increased. In an article for *Leslie's*, Harriet reported that it was no longer a novel sight to see a slender young girl piloting a powerful runabout through the congested traffic of a city's street, or a heavy touring car guided by a feminine hand. She wrote that milady had come to the conclusion that carburetor trouble was just as fashionable as appendicitis and a great deal more enjoyable.

In another article for *Leslie's*, Harriet wrote:

> The advantages of motoring are, of course, numerous and important. The automobile enlarges one's social circle to almost any radius of miles. To attend a luncheon twenty miles away is nothing. It places business, amusement, and education anywhere within a thousand miles within comparatively easy reach, which with a horse would be quite out of the question. It has been said by enthusiasts that an automobilist lives twice as much in the same span of years and increases his acquaintances, interests, and general knowledge to thrice the extent of the man without a motor wagon. When the motoring mania takes by storm the farmer as it has the city man, it will be a means of a social and industrial revolution throughout the country. (*Leslie's Illustrated Weekly*, 1906)

SOCIAL ISSUES ADVOCATE

By 1911, Harriet was quick to point out in her articles the increase in women drivers. She expressed her pleasure in the driving "academies" opening around the city where women were now admitted to learn not only how to drive, but to "tend" to their automobiles. Citing how in the past women had been victimized by unscrupulous mechanics, Harriet reported that women drivers who were not afraid to get their hands greasy and faces smudged could no longer be fooled by a chauffeur or charged for unnecessary repairs.

Times were changing, but not without resistance. The evolving role of women brought strong opinions as to why things should remain the same. A woman's primary role in the first decade of the twentieth century was to bear children and nurture her family. *Leslie's* reported on this changing tide, albeit often with mixed messages. In one editorial entitled "Either Business or Home, But Not Both," the editor began, "Is a woman naturally unsuited for the business world and does it age her prematurely?" Although the writer acknowledged that women in the business world was a phenomenon here to stay, he cautioned that they should not try to fill a business position and run a home simultaneously, as such double work would be too much for any woman—or even a man.

Many women openly rebelled against this type of thinking and paid the consequences. In 1908, one Kate Mulcahey was arrested in New York for smoking a cigarette in public, a violation of the Sullivan Smoking Act prohibiting such "unladylike" acts in public places. The judge fined her $5 and sentenced her to one night in jail. It should be noted that Harriet, too, was known to smoke cigarettes—and cigars—but never publicly. Because of the highly guarded distinction between her professional and private image, any behavior that could be remotely considered scandalous occurred only with her closest confidants.

As America industrialized and the need for workers increased, women and children came to be looked upon as a source for cheap labor. Both were exploited, hired for the most menial of tasks for which they were grossly underpaid, if paid at all. Such circumstances and a divided public provided Harriet with much to write about. Many of her articles focused on the unsafe working environments and sweatshop conditions endured by women in New York.

On March 25, 1911, one of the most horrific industrial tragedies in history took place at the Triangle Waist Company, then known as the Asch Building on Washington Place in Greenwich Village. Company owners had locked the doors and stairwells of the factory that manufactured men's shirts and employed mostly women and children. Locking the doors was a common practice to prevent employee pilfering and attempts to abandon the deplorable working conditions and twelve to fourteen-hour days. The building's one fire escape could not accommodate the 123 women, ranging in age from fourteen to forty-four, trying to escape the seething heat. Many workers leapt to their deaths from the ten-story building. Others were burned beyond recognition and found within the building's charred remains. Harriet fought with her pen to raise public awareness of unsafe work conditions and the rights of women and children. This was a major theme in all of her work.

Harriet was adept at her work and highly respected by her professional male colleagues. She thrived as the center of attention in which she often found herself. Remarkably, she was never a public target for acrimonious or jealous attacks from anyone, male or female, despite the controversial topics she wrote about. Suitors continued to pursue her, but Harriet never openly acknowledged a romantic relationship with any man or woman. John Sleicher, one of her editors at *Leslie's*, was from a prominent New

York family and the uncle of Caroline Vanderbilt, who married Earl Vanderbilt in 1909 and was tragically widowed eleven months later. Like Linda Griffith, Carrie Vanderbilt also became Harriet's close friend and traveling companion. There was no question that Harriet had a close relationship with the entire Sleicher family. In her will, written in 1909, Harriet designated John Sleicher as the executor of her estate. Sadly, just two years later he was faced with the task of burying Harriet using the $4,800 in her estate at the time of her death.

Later, even as her reputation as a flyer grew, Harriet maintained her aura of mystique. Fliers were famous for their wild exploits in the air, which were often matched by their personal escapades. Aviator Theodore Gordon Ellyson (USN), affectionately known as Spuds, was a member of an exclusive club frequented by aviators, including Harriet and her friend Matilde Moisant. After her death, Ellyson recalled evenings spent with Harriet, smoking, drinking, and exchanging flying stories. It is behavior that Harriet would likely not have admitted to.

> *"Where there is intellect, no face, however irregular the features,*
> *is entirely devoid of charm." —Harriet Quimby*

FROM JOURNALISM TO THEATER

Harriet's old acting friend from San Francisco, Linda Arvidson, followed the love of her life, David Wark Griffith (D. W. as he came to be known), to Boston after the 1906 earthquake. They married in 1907 and made their way to New York to seek their fortunes on the Broadway stage. Success was not initially forthcoming even though their circle of friends included famed producer David Belasco. The couple lived in near squalor and their situation became desperate enough that they turned to the only work they could get: the lowbrow business of silent films.

Harriet, now a popular journalist and Manhattan celebrity, offered to help in any way she could. In her biography written years later, Linda Griffith wrote that D. W. was quite jealous one day when Harriet, handsomely dressed and on her way to visit friends for dinner at a beach hotel, stopped by their flat to see how things were going. Fate would soon change the fortunes of the would-be director-producer, but on that day fame seemed a distant dream.

After a year as a struggling actor in New York, Griffith swallowed his disdain for the fledging movie industry and attempted to sell a script to Edison Studios head producer Edwin Porter. Porter rejected the script but offered Griffith a part in *Rescued from an Eagle's Nest*, Griffith's first foray into what he referred to as the "fly-by-night" motion picture business (Henderson, 1970). To his surprise, the actor found himself captivated. In 1908, when American Mutoscope & Biograph Company, commonly known as Biograph Studios, offered him another acting job, he was hooked.

Founded in 1895, Biograph was the first company in the United States devoted solely to film production. For almost three decades, it remained one of the most prolific studios, releasing over 3,000 short films and twelve feature films. When Biograph's premier director Wallace McCutcheon grew ill, his son, William, took his place. He failed miserably. Studio head Henry Marvin then handed the position to a rather surprised Griffith and a career that would span nearly fifty years was born. After Griffith's passing in 1948 at the Knickerbocker Hotel in Los Angeles, Charles Chaplin hailed his friend as "the teacher of all of us," a sentiment echoed by Alfred Hitchcock, John Ford, Cecil B. DeMille, and other great directors of the twentieth century (Henderson, 1970). None of this could have been predicted in 1908, when Griffith earned his first directing accolades with the release of *Judith of Bethulia*. When Griffith's career took off, so did his wife's. Linda would star in many of her husband's films, before and after their divorce, along with other famous celebrities of the time. Mary Pickford, Lillian and Dorothy Gish, Mack Sennett, and Lionel Barrymore all got their start at Biograph under Griffith's capable direction.

Harriet was thrilled for her friends and helped support the couple's growing success with articles in *Leslie's* describing how movies were made, accompanied by her photos of actors and set designs. She introduced the Griffiths to her editor, who declared his support for moving pictures. The paper's substantive reviews helped to advance the emerging industry, then considered no more than pornographic peep shows.

Biograph's acting crew wore many hats, including writing movie scripts, typically eighteen-minute shorts for which they were paid $10–$30. Scripts were narrative in style, vague in plot, and ran approximately thirty pages long.

Harriet never disclosed her personal connection to the Griffiths or Biograph Studios in her reporting for *Leslie's*. However, it was widely known that between 1909 and 1911, Biograph released seven romantic film shorts with screenplay credits attributed to Harriet Quimby. They include *The Broken Cross, His Mother's Scarf, In the Days of '49, A Smile of a Child, The Blind Princess and the Poet, Sunshine Through the Dark,* and *Fisher Folks.* Biograph stars Florence La Badie, Wilfred Lucas, and Blanche Sweet were featured players in the films, directed by Griffith. Either for pay or on a lark, Harriet made a brief appearance as an extra in *Fisher Folks,* which also starred Linda Griffith. Harriet's interest in the fishing industry may have begun along the shores of Lake Michigan where she spent her early years. She had previously written an article for *Call* entitled "A Day with the Fishermen." Ironically because of what was to come, water always held a romance and mystique for her and most likely inspired her writing this first script for her friend.

The films she wrote for Biograph Studios can be found today in the silent film archives at the Metropolitan Museum of Art in New York City. Although Harriet's scripts are credited to her, it was not common practice to give screen credit to any writer or production staff. One can only speculate about why Griffith chose to credit Harriet, but as a result, she is recognized as the first publicly acknowledged female screenwriter in the country.

It was rumored that Harriet was torn between her love for her friend Linda Griffith and her admiration and love for Linda's husband. Her close connection to both continued until Harriet's death. They did not socialize often, especially when Harriet's interests moved toward flying. However, while traveling in Egypt, Harriet, who often bought souvenir jewelry and good luck trinkets for herself, purchased a large, intricate scarab ring for D. W. Though known for his distaste for wearing jewelry, including a wedding ring, the scarab appeared in photographs of the director through the years. Linda remained loyal to Harriet, even accompanying her to Dover, England, for her flight across the English Channel, where she proudly presented the aviatrix with a carnation and ceremonial kiss for good luck. The depth of Harriet's relationship with Linda and D. W. was never revealed.

"The value of moving pictures as an aid to historians cannot be overestimated."—Harriet Quimby

D. W. Griffith and Linda (Arvidson) Griffith about the time they met in San Francisco between 1900 and 1903. Both remained life-long friends of Harriet. Museum of Modern Art, New York City.

German photographer Arnold Genthe
introduced Harriet to the camera,
which she often used in her career as a
photojournalist. Library of Congress,
Genthe Collection.

Nude photo of Harriet taken by
Arnold Genthe. It hung above the bar
in San Francisco's famed Bohemian
Club until the 1906 earthquake leveled
the city. Library of Congress.

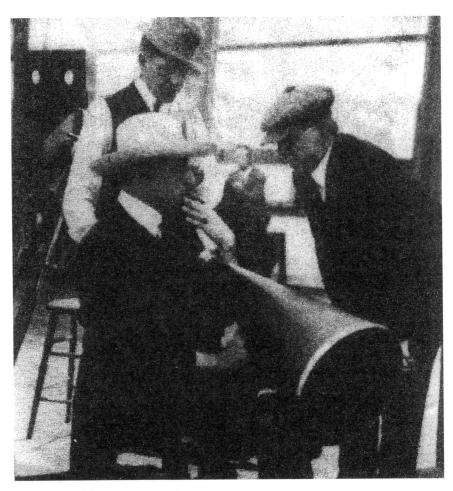

D. W. Griffith did not wear any jewelry except
the large scarab ring from Harriet. He wore it
until his death in 1948. From *D. W. Griffith,
The Years at Biograph*, Robert M. Henderson.

The Quimby family's rock farm in Coldwater,
Michigan, where Harriet was born May 11,
1875. Library of Congress.

Bohemian Club members at the time Harriet was a member (from left: Porter Garnette, George Sterling, and Jack London). Library of Congress.

Frank Leslie, founder and publisher of *Leslie's Illustrated Weekly*. The newspaper was Harriet's home base from 1903 until her death in 1912. She wrote over 250 articles for the publication, serving as its first drama critic, first foreign correspondent, and first photojournalist. Library of Congress.

Frank Leslie's wife, Miriam Florence Leslie, a prominent suffrage leader of the time who worked with her husband at *Leslie's Illustrated Weekly* from its inception in 1852. She continued its operation after her husband's death in 1880, selling the illustrious publication in 1902. Library of Congress.

Penn Station at the time Harriet arrived in New
York City. Archives of the *Pittsburgh Post-Gazette*.

Leslie's
ILLUSTRATED WEEKLY
THE OLDEST ILLUSTRATED WEEKLY NEWSPAPER IN THE UNITED STATES

New York Office: Brunswick Building, 225 Fifth Avenue. Western Advertising Office: Marquette Building, Chicago, Ill.; Washington Representative, Munsey Building, Washington, D. C.

Branch Subscription Offices in thirty-seven cities of the United States.

European Agents: The International News Company, Bream's Building, Chancery Lane, E C London, England; Smithson's News Exchange, 36 John Street, Adelphi, London; 36 Rue de la Victoire Paris; 1 Carn Strasse, Mainz, Germany; Brentano's, Avenue de l'Opera, Paris, France.

Subscriptions and advertising for all the publications of Leslie-Judge Company will be taken at regular rates at any of the above offices.

Persons representing themselves as connected with LESLIE'S should always be asked to produce credentials.

TO ADVERTISERS. — Our circulation books are open for your inspection.

TERMS: Ten cents a copy, $5.00 a year, to all subscribers in the United States, Mexico, Hawaii, Porto Rico, the Philippine Islands, Guam, Tutuila, Samoa. Foreign postage, $1.50 extra. Twelve cents per copy, $6.00 per year, to Canadian subscribers. Subscriptions are payable in advance by draft on New York, or by express or postal money order. BACK NUMBERS: Present year, 10 cents per copy; 1910, 20 cents; 1909, 30 cents, etc.

Subscribers when ordering a change of address should give the old as well as the new address, and the larger number on their wrapper. From two to three weeks must necessarily elapse before the change can be made.

Subscribers to Preferred List (see Jasper's column in this issue) will get current issue always.

The publishers will be glad to hear from subscribers who have just cause for complaint. If LESLIE'S cannot be found at any news-stand, the publishers would be under obligations if that fact be promptly reported. Senders of photographs or letterpress must always include return postage. We receive such material only on condition that we shall not be held responsible for loss or injury while in our hands or in transit.

CONTENTS

WHO'S WHO ON THE RIALTO.
82. ANNIE RUSSELL, IN "THE STRONGER SEX,"
AT WEBER'S.
Caricature by E. A. Goewey.

(left) *Leslie's Illustrated Weekly*, **June 23, 1910** "Why New York Laughs at Marie Dressler," by Harriet Quimby and other reviews featured such stars as Annie Russell (above).

Table of contents from an issue of *Leslie's Illustrated Weekly*, showing one of Harriet's early bylines for *Leslie's Illustrated Weekly*. Library of Congress.

30

Harriet Quimby, the belle of
Manhattan. Library of Congress.

Harriet in her yellow roadster, which she drove to local assignments for *Leslie's Illustrated Weekly.* Library of Congress.

In "Automobiling, the Society Woman's Latest Fad" (*Leslie's Weekly*, January 26, 1905), Harriet wrote that it was "no longer a novelty to see a sixteen-horsepower machine making its way through a crowded thoroughfare under the sole guidance of a woman." Library of Congress.

Biograph Studios at 11 East Fourteenth
Street in New York, where Harriet
contributed seven film narratives for
Griffith. From *D. W. Griffith, The Years at
Biograph*, by Robert M. Henderson.

Released February 16, 1911

FISHER FOLKS

No matter how homely the exterior a pure soul will so light up a personality that the plain personal appearance will be obliterated in its radiance. True love is born of the soul, hence it is stable, but love induced by personal appearance is as transitory as winds, changing with each new attraction. In this Biograph subject the line is clearly drawn comparing the two, with fate a controlling power. Steve Hardester, a handsome young fisherman, is infatuated with Cora, the village flirt. She, though really caring for him, must indulge her inclination to coquetry, laughingly flinging love back into his face, often making him the target of derision. Our story opens on the day of the Fair in the little fishing village. Bertha, a poor cripple, with a slightly deformed figure, but a pure sweet face, being too frail to undergo the toil of the fishergirl, ekes a livelihood selling flowers to to the gallant fisherboys with which to deck their sweethearts' tresses. On this day Bertha starts out long before daybreak to gather the dewy blossoms and form them into nosegays for sale to the young swains before the opening of the Fair. This done long before the dawn, she reclines on the beach and dozes off through sheer fatigue and sleeps until the morning sun awakens her. Going through the village she meets Steve as he is about to enter his cottage. Offering her bouquets, he purchases one to give to the object of his affection, Cora. Sad of heart, poor Bertha wishes she had some one to show her those little attentions, particularly Steve, as she has always loved the handsome young fisherman. Cora, though, imagining that she can have her choice of the boys on account of her attractiveness, takes delight in holding Steve's little favors up to ridicule and this occasion is no exception, for when he invites her to attend the Fair and presents her with the bunch of wild flowers, she pokes fun at it. This is the last straw and Steve snatches the flowers from her and crushes them under his heel, leaving her for good. This at first amuses Cora for she thinks herself irresistible and he will come back. But not so, for as he dashes back to his cottage he meets again the little flower seller. Her sweet face now appeals to him and in a moment of pique through wounded pride, rather than a tender feeling for Bertha, he asks her to attend the Fair with him. Her joy is ecstatic at this and she and Steve make their way to the fair grounds, much to the chagrin of Cora, who has from a distance witnessed their meeting. However, Cora assumes an indifferent mien, feeling that Steve's action is induced by a spirit of revenge. This is at first true, but Steve's association with Bertha cultivates something more serious. He now realizes the worth of an affection born of a pure soul, and they become betrothed, their marriage following shortly after. Cora is now the one to suffer wounded pride. She realizes she has lost the best catch in the village, and to one whom she regards as so inferior. Obsessed by a desire for revenge she determines at any cost to wreak it. Some time later she visits the young couple's cottage, ostensibly to congratulate them, but upon leaving slips a note to Steve to meet her at the old trysting place. More than mere curiosity impels him to see her and on the eve of his departure on a long cruise he is there to bid her an adieu. More than a year passes and no word comes from the fishing crew, until late one afternoon their vessel is seen in the distance slowly nearing the shore. The little village is at once alive with excitement. Kindly fishermen inform Bertha of the approach of the long absent fisher crew and she takes up her little charge, which had arrived in the meantime, to make her way as fast as possible to the landing place. Her heart is almost bursting with joy in the anticipation of Steve's surprise when she places in his arms their little son. But what grief awaits her, for Cora arriving first lures him off to her cottage, Bertha arriving just in time to see them going hurriedly up the beach. Almost heartbroken and forlorn she wends her way homeward when at a turn in the lane she comes face to face with Steve. What a shock. He now realizes what a contemptible brute he is and so has not the heart to face her. Bertha, however, has nothing but forgiveness and love portrayed in her countenance so Steve takes the little one from her outstretched arms and together they go to their humble cottage, leaving Cora transfixed with suppressed rage on the sands.

APPROXIMATE LENGTH 998 FEET   **NO. 3787**   **CODE WORD—RHIANOS**

Produced and Controlled Exclusively by

BIOGRAPH COMPANY

11 East 14th Street, New York City.

GEORGE KLEINE   SELLING AGENT FOR CHICAGO
52 STATE STREET,   CHICAGO, ILL.

Handbill for Fisher Folks, first of seven screenplay treatments Harriet wrote for her friend D. W. Griffith at Biograph. He acknowledged her work (documented in *D. W. Griffith, The Years at Biograph*), making her the first credited female scriptwriter in the United States. *Motion Picture World* and *Motion Picture Magazine*, Academy of Motion Pictures Arts and Sciences, Margaret Herrick Library Department of Special Collections, Los Angeles.

IN THE DAYS OF '49

An Episode in the Times of the Gold Fever

DURING that exciting period men were wont to rush from place to place in their mad lust for gold, and Bill Weston was one of these, who, after locating with his wife in one settlement, goes off to another where the chances seem better, intending to send for her if he strikes luck. He hits it fairly well and so sends a letter telling his wife to take the first coach out, which she does. On the way she meets handsome Jack, the gambler, who, riding on the same coach, deeply impresses her with his attentions. When she meets her husband, who is but a plain honest fellow, she compares the two, and Jack finds it easy to induce her to meet him later and go away. Bill feels his wife's coolness towards him and is grief stricken, telling the boys of the camp that his wife does not love him. Jack sees his plight and realizes what a great wrong he is working so he goes away leaving a note advising the wife, "Don't be a fool. Appreciate a good man's love while you have it. Go back to your husband who loves you with a better love." The wife at this is also awakened.

BIOGRAPH

Released May 8, 1911

Handbill for *In the Days of '49*, screenplay by Harriet for Biograph Studios. *Motion Picture World* and *Motion Picture Magazine*, Academy of Motion Picture Arts and Sciences, Margaret Herrick Library Department of Special Collections, Los Angeles.

THE BROKEN CROSS

An Experience of a Country Boy in the City

A COUNTRY BOY on leaving his little sweetheart on his departure for the city to seek his fortune plights his troth. The girl breaks in two a cross giving him one half as a love token agreeing that if either wishes to break the engagement he or she will send back the piece. In the city a manicure girl becomes impressed with him and tries to win him for herself by sending him a piece of broken cross purporting to come from his country girl sweetheart. Her scheme at first seems to be successful, but he discovers the parts do not match and so, disgusted with the falseness of city living, goes back to the country and his little sweetheart.

 **BIOGRAPH**

Released April 6, 1911

Handbill for *The Broken Cross*, screenplay by Harriet
for Biograph Studios. *Motion Picture World* and
Motion Picture Magazine, Academy of Motion
Pictures Arts and Sciences, Margaret Herrick Library
Department of Special Collections, Los Angeles.

HIS MOTHER'S SCARF

Now It Served as a Peacemaker

THE MORAL of this Biograph subject is the power of a mother's love. Two brothers out in the wilds of the Western hills, meet and fall in love with a young girl, who was the sole survivor of an Indian outrage. Through jealousy one brother is about to annihilate the other when the sight of a scarf, the present from their mother, now dead, awakens his better self. The scenic beauty of this production has never been equaled.

Ⓐ BIOGRAPH Ⓑ

Released April 24, 1911

Handbill for *His Mother's Scarf*, screenplay by Harriet for Biograph Studios. *Motion Picture World* and *Motion Picture Magazine*, Academy of Motion Pictures Arts and Sciences, Margaret Herrick Library Department of Special Collections, Los Angeles.

A SMILE OF A CHILD

THE INNOCENT smile of a child has more influence than any other power in the world. It can change the cloudy into sunshine as will be seen in this Biograph subject. An ill-tempered Prince is met by a little child who is wandering through his grounds, and his entire nature is changed into one of excessive good nature. Later, while out on a lark, he meets for the first time a very pretty peasant woman, to whom he, by virtue of his rank, makes sinister advances. It happens that she is the mother of the same child and it enters in time to arouse the Prince to his better self with its sunny smile and saucy wink, which wink is really infectious of good nature.

Ⓐ BIOGRAPH Ⓑ

Released June 5, 1911

Handbill for *A Smile of a Child*, screenplay by Harriet for Biograph Studios. *Motion Picture World* and *Motion Picture Magazine*, Academy of Motion Picture Arts and Sciences, Margaret Herrick Library Department of Special Collections, Los Angeles.

THE BLIND PRINCESS
AND THE POET

A Biograph Fantasy In the Land of Flowers

T HE BLIND PRINCESS upon consulting the soothsayer is told that upon the first kiss of unselfish love she receives she will see. All the great lords assemble to pay her court and bestow kisses in hopes of restoring her sight. There are Lords Gold, Selfish, Folly, Presumption and their ilk, but their attentions are in vain. A poor Poet has humbly loved the Princess, but considers himself unworthy until the Child Equality argues differently. Lord Gold in rage kills the Child Equality and the Poet loses hope. However, when the Princess sleeps the poor Poet steals a kiss. The Princess sees, and through the Poet's kiss. Lord Selfish would kill the Poet but he is thwarted by Justice, as the Poet goes singing to his apparent death. Justice takes him to the Princess' side.

 BIOGRAPH

Released Aug. 17, 1911

Handbill for *The Blind Princess and the Poet*, screenplay by
Harriet for Biograph Studios. *Motion Picture World* and
Motion Picture Magazine, Academy of Motion Picture
Arts and Sciences, Margaret Herrick Library Department
of Special Collections, Los Angeles.

SUNSHINE
THROUGH THE DARK

The Little Slavey Finds the Silver Lining to the Cloud of Despair

THE poor little housemaid, with her tired hands incessantly toiling, despairs of ever experiencing a kindness, for although she reproves herself for complaining, having what she deems a good job, still her life is that of one driven like a beast of burden. Even the spoiled child of the household orders her about and treats her with absolute disdain. The child wears a bright ribbon sash, which to the poor eyes of the slavey is overwhelmingly beautiful; so much so that she is tempted to steal it. She has it in her possession but a few minutes, when she reproaches herself and starts to return it. But, meanwhile, her act has been discovered and she is denounced as a thief. This is done in the presence of her sweetheart, the stable boy, who at first turns from her, but finally realizing the act was one of impulsiveness, forgives her and takes her to his heart.

 BIOGRAPH

Released Nov. 27, 1911

Handbill for *Sunshine Through the Dark*, screenplay by Harriet for Biograph Studios. *Motion Picture World* and *Motion Picture Magazine*, Academy of Motion Picture Arts and Sciences, Margaret Herrick Library Department of Special Collections, Los Angeles. All seven scripts were released between February and November 1911.

Chapter Four

THE AVIATRIX (1910–1912)

"I would never give up my work for flying. I care too much for my work. And a business woman cannot really want more notoriety."
—Harriet Quimby

Harriet was always looking for something exciting to share with her readers, and there was little she wouldn't explore to satisfy her sense of adventure. In early 1910, she was about to discover perhaps her greatest passion, which would also test the endurance of the American male's Victorian values.

On October 31, 1910, her friend Matilde Moisant invited her to attend the Statue of Liberty Race at Belmont Park race track. During the dawn of aviation in the United States, horse racing parks served as natural "aerodomes." One of the more prominent was Belmont Park on Long Island, New York. Known today as "the championship trail" since nearly every winning thoroughbred in twentieth-century racing history has competed there, Belmont first opened its gates to horse racing in 1896. Beginning in 1910, aviation racing for substantial prize money was held at Belmont and what was then called Hemstead Plains, until New York State banned such exhibitions two years later. On this crisp fall day, Matilde Moisant's brother John would fly the graceful Bleriot XI monoplane, competing against several European aviators for a $10,000 purse.

This was America's second air show. The first had occurred ten months earlier at Dominquez Field (now the city of Carson a few miles south of Los Angeles), where it had attracted over 250,000 spectators to what was hailed as an overwhelming aeronautics extravaganza. Harriet had represented *Leslie's* at this event, filing a report on a Japanese aeronaut competing in his first exhibition. In her August 5, 1909, article "A Japanese Aeronaut to Startle the World," Harriet quoted the Japanese pilot who claimed that "the flight pattern of the American buzzard combined with Japanese ingenuity would lead the evolution of aeronautics worldwide." That remained to be seen. The popular idea at the time was that an air machine required at least two wings of square design held together with glue and wires. This biplane design, created by Wilbur and Orville Wright, was considered the ideal. John Moisant's single-wing monoplane, however, was supported by the European community and thought by this emerging minority to be the real future of aviation design.

Harriet was no stranger to Belmont Park. It was a jet set destination for everyone who was anyone in society and now aviation had arrived at Belmont, making it the place to gather and be seen. John Moisant, however, was a mystery to her, despite her friendship with his sister. He had a checkered career history as an aeronautical engineer, business entrepreneur, aviator, flight instructor, and, of particular interest to Harriet, a revolutionary. This dapper "king of aviators," as he was known, funded his aviation passion from successful business ventures in El Salvador, where he had led two failed revolutions and coup attempts against then President Eduardo Figueroa (*Air Force Magazine*, 1960). El Salvador was a long way from Kankakee, Illinois, where Moisant was born in 1868 to French-Canadian immigrants. He and two of his brothers made their way to Central America in 1896 to purchase sugar cane plantations that, within a short time, generated substantial sums of money to support his family back home. The young American's business acumen so impressed El Salvador's new president, Jose Santos Celaya, that he asked the young man to represent his country at a conference in France, where the legitimacy of the aeroplane would be the topic of international discussion.

What began as a hobby—like his soon-to-be pupil Harriet Quimby, he was open to adventure—now became his new frontier. He designed and built two aircraft in 1910, even before becoming a licensed pilot. His first, the Moisant biplane, was an experimental plane built in Paris's famous Clement-Bayard factory. It was the first all-metal aircraft in the world, constructed entirely from aluminum and steel. The biplane's inaugural flight (and Moisant's first flight) early that same year resulted in a crash landing after rising just ninety feet above the ground.

Undaunted, Moisant built a second model, a monoplane. Its flawed design made it impossible for the craft to rest upright on the ground. It never left the runway.

Moisant then turned his attention from designing aircraft to flying them. He studied with the renowned Louis Bleriot, who owned a flight school outside Paris and was the first French inventor and design engineer to build and fly a pilot-powered monoplane. Moisant learned his lessons well. Harriet and the other spellbound onlookers watched in awe at the Belmont International Tournament that morning as he circled the Bleriot XI around a marker balloon over ten miles away and returned to the racetrack in just thirty-nine minutes. Although Americans favored the Wright biplanes with a set of wings above and below the fuselage, Moisant was out to prove that the Bleriot-type monoplane, with its single set of wings above the plane's skeleton, was the design of the future. He conducted the first passenger flights across the English Channel from Paris to London, and in this country throughout Mississippi, where his Moisant International Aviators or the flying circus, as he called it, was headquartered.

With her sense for detail, Harriet studied the sky filled with biplanes, monoplanes, dirigibles, and even balloons, looping and darting about in strange yet fascinating configurations. She knew flying was still considered pure entertainment, with crowds fully prepared to see fiery crashes and bodies plunging to the ground. Maybe it was the thrill of watching her friend's brother demonstrate the artistry of flight and making it appear effortless that led her to tell Matilde, "It really looks quite easy. I believe I can do it myself—and I will" (*Leslie's Illustrated Weekly*, 1911). A new fire had ignited in her heart.

Matilde understood perfectly, for she, too, was an aviatrix at heart even though her brothers, including John, tried to dampen her enthusiasm. Matilde reminded her friend that it was 1910. Men did not want women driving even a motorcar. Could Harriet possibly see them supporting female pilots?

Her friend's words seemed incredulous to Harriet, since Matilde's own brothers, John and Alfred, had recently opened the Moisant Aviation School in Mineola, practically next store to Belmont racetrack. However, she did know that Orville Wright had rejected all female applicants when he and Wilbur opened their flight school in Alabama. Their reasoning, they explained to aspiring students, was based on the belief that women who wanted to fly were simply seeking notoriety. The Wright brothers also argued that aviation was a man's game, due to economic factors more than social bias. They explained that women earned considerably less than their male counterparts. Flying lessons could cost up to $1,000 (approximately $3 per lesson), more than even many men earned in a year. They had even refused to teach their sister Katherine, who wanted desperately to fly her own plane. The popular brothers would cling to their cavalier attitude until the times, and women like Harriet Quimby, finally changed the national consensus.

Over dinner at the Hotel Astor the evening after Moisant's victory in the Statue of Liberty Race, Harriet and Matilde convinced Moisant, his brother Alfred, and balloonist A. Leo Stevens to admit them to the new Moisant Aviation School. Stevens would come to play an important role in Harriet's life as her mentor, manager, and rumored lover. The three men agreed, with one stipulation: With winter's fast approach, they would have to wait until spring. Besides, Moisant told them, he was about to head south to compete in air exhibitions promoting the Bleriot XI monoplane. Patience was a virtue of neither Harriet nor Matilde, but both promised to wait until his return in May.

Harriet initially decided not to inform her editors at *Leslie's* about her new passion. She continued to file in-depth reports on poverty, child labor abuses, and industrial mistreatment that debilitated women and children in New York City. She also continued to cover the Broadway theater beat and file travel stories, all the while keeping her sights on spring and the vision of seeing herself in the cockpit. Harriet had fallen in love with the monoplane. Its sleek, bird-like design complemented her sense of style. She even thought about prerequisites for prospective student pilots, telling friends that anyone who has driven a motorcycle or automobile is all the more qualified to begin flight lessons. Without this type of experience, she added, the noise of an unmuffled aeroplane motor would be utterly nerve-racking.

On December 31, 1910, Harriet was shocked to learn that John Moisant had been killed in Kenner, Louisiana, just outside New Orleans. He was participating in the Michelin Cup race in hopes of securing the $4,000 prize. As he prepared to land, his beloved Bleriot XI caught a strong wind gust that ejected him from the plane. The crowd watched in horror as he plummeted headfirst to the ground. Moisant, the self-promoting entrepreneur who had developed a reputation for flamboyance, who had shocked his European contemporaries and the public with his cavalier attitude toward danger, died on impact at age forty-one. This "birdman-hero," as Harriet called him, was as close to a role model as Harriet would ever have (*Leslie's Illustrated Weekly*, 1911).

"Flying is a fine, dignified sport for women. It is healthy and stimulates the mind." —Harriet Quimby

Badly shaken by his brother's death, Alfred Moisant thought seriously about closing the Moisant Aviation School. However, he recognized that American aviation lagged far beyond its European counterparts and he wanted to raise its status in the US. After much soul searching, Alfred decided not to close the school.

Matilda's two other remaining brothers, however, adamantly opposed the idea of Matilda learning to fly. Harriet's long-suffering father was heard from, too, writing to his daughter from California that women did not belong in aviation or in any other man's activity. Those were fighting words to Harriet. She did receive support from her mother, who, though she thought flying quite dangerous, believed women had a right to pursue it. Mr. Quimby knew he was wasting his breath. On May 10, 1911, one day before her thirty-sixth birthday, Harriet joined Matilde and three male classmates at the school on Nassau Boulevard. Harriet's destiny had taken yet another turn.

Because of the social pressures on women aviators, Harriet and Matilde Moisant disguised themselves as men for their lessons at sunrise each morning. Harriet drove from her Manhattan apartment to the flying field before dawn. Professional as always, she did not want to jeopardize her reporting duties and, more important, attract any attention that might embarrass her bosses at *Leslie's*. Besides, she loved the crispness and calmness of the air in those early morning hours.

Though expensive, flight school in 1911 was not complicated. The first week paralleled today's "ground school," with instruction devoted to daily lectures on flight theory and airplane construction. Laboratory work comprised the second week of training. Students dismantled, then reassembled, various parts, including the motor, while familiarizing themselves with the purpose of each. By the third week, students had the opportunity to experience the plane through simulation technology. They were introduced to a plane similar to one they would eventually fly, but which was bolted to the hanger floor. This prototype could simulate a flight to some degree. One could "feel" the engine and propeller power and the rush of air. In addition, controls could be manipulated without serious consequences. During the fourth week of flight training, the fledgling pilots were introduced to a state-of-the-art training aircraft. Heavy, well-built, and designed to fly no higher than two or three feet off the ground, this phase of training focused on how to maneuver the machine in a straight line over a grass strip. In reality, mastery was defined as the ability to do so in any way approximating a straight line. Harriet was quoted as saying, "This looks quite easy, until one discovers that an aeroplane has the perversity common to all inanimate objects. It persists in moving the other way, instead of the way you seek to direct it. Your first dash across the field and back takes two minutes *if* no mishap occurs. If you're successful after two attempts, a discreet teacher elects to dismiss you for the day, for you surely have endured all your nerves should be asked to stand" (*New York Times*, 1911).

After a student successfully drove a straight line six or seven times, he or she then was asked to conduct short hops of two or three feet into the air and across the field, a skill newspaper reporters referred to as kangarooing. Harriet noticed that it was not unusual for students, including herself, to forget the instructions to not inadvertently shift the elevator lever. If shot too quickly into the air, startled pilots would find themselves higher than anticipated. The immediate reaction to seek a sudden descent would result not only in dreaded "breakage," but considerable embarrassment. Breakage was a term Harriet coined, and it remained a serious problem for these fragile wooden planes (*Leslie's Illustrated Weekly*, 1911). So much so that in addition to the expense of lessons, students paid a $1,000–1,500 deposit to offset any damage they caused during the five-week training program.

Once students mastered steering the aircraft, they moved into the final week. In what was called the "supervised solo," the fledgling flyer was expected to make a series of supervised "jumps." For this test, a special device fitted to the airplane's tail limited its altitude (Holden, 1993).

After successfully completing the five-week program and deemed prepared to test, the student at last settled into the thirty-horsepower Moisant-built monoplane, which was sturdier than most planes of that era. It was an impressive machine with its fuselage of spruce, a landing chassis of hickory, and its cradle constructed from bamboo. High-grade piano wire secured the wooden parts, and imported French three-ply rubber-impregnated silk spread across the wing and tail. The propeller was carved from solid laminated mahogany. Missing was any suggestion of a windshield to protect pilots from the propeller's blast, making visibility a persistent problem. Goggles coated with dust, dirt, oil, and insects seriously impaired a pilot's vision during flight. Then there was the slight quirk found in the rotary engine, what some pilots referred to as "looseness in the lower gut" (Holden, 1993). As Harriet reported in one of her articles for *Leslie's*, "Not only are the chassis and all fixtures slippery with lubricating oil, but when the engine picks up speed, a shower of oil is thrown back into the pilot's face—it is interesting that this lubricating oil is castor."

Most engines used mineral oil as a lubricant, but in a rotary engine, oil and fuel commingled in the hollow crank shaft. Vegetable oil did not break down when exposed to the fuel, so castor oil was the chosen substitute. Any unburned castor oil sprayed from the valves in a fine mist, creating a murky film that coated everything. Inhaling the gluey substance could be equated to sniffing toxic epoxy.

Still, Harriet was hooked. Despite the fragile construction of airplanes, the temperamental nature of engines, not to mention unpredictable weather, Harriet's pre-license record was nearly perfect. Only once, while attempting takeoff during her last week of training, did a slight mishap occur. One of her plane's wheels hit a gopher hole. The bicycle-size disk detached from the craft and careened into the wing, breaking it to bits. Harriet remained composed. She calmly shut off the engine, climbed from the plane, and walked back to the starting point. Seemingly unruffled and ever confident, she asked for another aircraft to try again.

It is not surprising that Harriet's lessons did not remain a secret for long. A *New York Times* reporter discovered her charade while visiting the airfield early one morning. Harriet knew the *Times* planned to publish an article dubbing her the Dresden China aviatrix. When the reporter asked if she enjoyed flying, she replied, "Do I like flying?! Well, I am out here at 4:00 a.m. each day. That ought to be answer enough. You see, motoring is all right, and I have done a lot of that. But after seeing monoplanes in the air, I couldn't resist the desire to try the air lanes where there are neither speed laws nor traffic policemen, and where one needn't go all the way around Central Park to get across Times Square ("Woman in Trousers One Daring Aviator," *New York Times*, May 11, 1911). She also informed the surprised reporter of her intention to become America's first licensed woman aviator.

Recognizing that the time had come to tell *Leslie's* about her new passion, Harriet shared the news of the upcoming *Times* article with her editors. They were not surprised, and Harriet was glad the charade had ended. Besides, she loved the publicity. *Leslie's* management welcomed Harriet's new venture with enthusiasm. This would create an exciting and controversial new subject for their most popular employee to write about. Most of the articles published had described air tragedies. Harriet's reporting of her first-hand experiences would whet the readers' sense of adventure and certainly increase subscriptions. That is exactly what happened. Before long, Harriet was receiving fan mail addressed to "our bird girl" (*New York Times*, May 11, 1911).

Leslie's first official acknowledgment of Harriet's foray into flying appeared in the May 25, 1911, article "How A Woman Learns to Fly." For her next article, "Exploring the Air Lanes," Harriet's editors prefaced the piece with "Miss Quimby, the dramatic critic of *Leslie's Weekly* and editor of its Women's Page, is the first woman to manipulate a monoplane. Two years ago, she became interested in the flight of buzzards. Miss Quimby wrote an article suggesting that in order for the aeroplane to be successful, it must be devised to imitate the buzzard's wing and tail [referring to Harriet's article "A Japanese Aeronaut to Startle the World"]. Miss Quimby has been making a careful study of aviation and will report the results of her interesting experiences in the air exclusively in upcoming issues of *Leslie's Weekly*."

In fact, *Leslie's* was so pleased with Harriet's latest venture that it agreed to reimburse her for flying lessons. Aviation was considered a dangerous, expensive pursuit, one left to daring young men and society ladies. Once again, Harriet defied the odds. She demonstrated a natural talent for flying and certainly the drive to prove that women could advance in the field as well as any man. "I'm going in for everything in aviation that men have done including altitude, speed, endurance, everything," she declared in one of her articles. Yet she remained distinctly feminine, stating in the same article, "You don't know what a fine thing for the complexion a dew bath is as you rise to the pure, moist air at altitude" (*Leslie's Illustrated Weekly*, 1911).

On the last day of July in 1911, after thirty-three flying lessons and less than five hours in the air, flight instructor Andre Houpert informed her she was ready to take the pilot's exam. It consisted of three parts: The first two required five alternate right and left turns around pylons and the completion of five figure-eights. The third portion was the landing test. Representatives from the Aero Club of America, the licensing agency in the United States for the Federation Aeronautique Internationale, facilitated all flight exams. It was no secret that officials were highly skeptical of a woman learning to fly and resisted making the trip to New York when they learned Harriet would be testing. Only when Houpert told them a male student, Ferdinand de Muria, was scheduled to test the same day did the officials agree to make the trip.

Harriet was annoyed by the skepticism, for she knew that she handled a plane better than most of her male counterparts. On exam day she smiled confidently at the judges as she shook their hands and made her way to her aircraft. She noted they did not smile back. Harriet completed the first two parts with ease. However, during the final stage of the test, she set the plane down too far from her landing point. Test regulations required a pilot to return the aircraft to within 100 feet from where the plane left the ground. According to Harriet, the Aero Club representatives seemed relieved that they did not have to issue the license. They were scheduled to return the following day to test Harriet's fellow student Ferdinand de Muria, and Houpert told Harriet not to be discouraged. He instructed his student to go home, review her performance, and return the next day for another try.

That evening, Harriet told Matilde that the test had not been difficult but that she had somehow miscalculated her landing. Matilde reassured her that she would certainly pass the next day. At Harriet's insistence, she also agreed to take the exam herself the next day so the two women could celebrate their victories together. Matilde insisted, however, that she would complete her exam only after Harriet had successfully achieved her goal. She said after Harriet's death that she had wanted her to enjoy the fame associated with being the first woman to earn her pilot's license. She knew that achieving this ambition would enhance Harriet's image and career.

The two met for breakfast at dawn the next morning. As they passed through the Garden City hotel lobby on their way to the restaurant, a desk clerk told Harriet that there was an urgent message from Houpert. The flying field was blanketed with fog, and she was not to report to the field until he advised her that flying conditions had improved.

As they ate breakfast, the two judges from Aero Club, also guests at the hotel, entered the dining room. To the men's obvious discomfort, Harriet greeted them enthusiastically. She was, she told them, prepared and eager to retake her exam that morning. They seemed incredulous. Why, they asked, would she want to test on a day when conditions were so poor? Why would she not consider waiting for another time, when she could really have the opportunity to demonstrate her flying prowess? As she had done so many times before, Harriet stared directly at the two. Smiling sweetly, she invited the men to drive with her and Matilde to the airfield. "Not the least bit encouraging were they," Harriet told friends later. "They were reserved and polite, but highly skeptical of both my, and Matilde's, intentions of passing the flight exam" (*New York Times*, 1911).

The men did not accompany Harriet and Matilde to the field. When they arrived, fog still hugged the ground and seemed to grow thicker the closer they got. Visibility was less than fifty feet. Harriet could see Houpert was irritated that she had disobeyed his instruction to wait. As midday approached and the fog still hung heavy over Hemstead Plains, even Harriet's smile waned. The only optimist in the group was the chief mechanic, who predicted the fog would lift within an hour. How he could tell this, Harriet never knew, but he was right. As noon drew near, the fog lifted on cue. Harriet's attention now turned to the tiny red flag waving wildly at the end of a bamboo pole in the middle of the airfield. The fog had lifted, but the wind had picked up considerably, casting further doubts about getting on with the test.

Using an anemometer, Houpert measured the wind's velocity. This small, hand-held instrument resembling a windmill, but with cups rather than blades, measured wind by the speed at which the cups revolved. If velocity registered at over five miles per hour, the test would be cancelled. Harriet understood that to fly into anything more than a five-mile-an-hour breeze in a low-powered monoplane was courting disaster. She remembered reporting once about another method to measure wind speed. She had followed the career of pilot Glenn Curtiss, who gauged air safety by cigar smoke. Though not a smoker himself, Harriet had explained in her story, Curtiss would distribute cigars noted for their heavy smoke to testers. They would light the cigars, tilt their heads skyward, and blow. If the smoke rose straight up, flying weather was good. Harriet's article had also disclosed, with an air of sarcasm, reports of a new advance in technology. Aviators could now simply pull a handkerchief from their pocket, extend it arm's length mid-air, and accurately judge the wind's velocity by the linen's fluttering intensity!

Whatever his testing method that day, Houpert returned to the assembled group and nodded to Harriet. She climbed into her single-seat aircraft. The crowd, which had gathered the previous morning to see a woman attempt to earn a pilot's license, had returned in even greater numbers. They watched in silence as Harriet checked her controls, which consisted of only a warping lever, a control stick, and rudder bars. The simple airplane lacked ailerons used to raise or lower the wings. Instead, Harriet would have to manually turn the stick that twisted the entire fragile wing.

She flipped the switch to start the battery and waved her arm high to signal the mechanic that it was time to engage the wooden propeller. As the spark plugs ignited and the propeller picked up speed, the fuel met the glow of the spark plugs' head and ignited the thirty-horsepower engine. The propeller whirled at 1,400 rpms as the engine's three cylinders coughed oil-filled smoke onto the ground crew straining to hold back the aircraft. When the smoke cleared, Harriet's smiling face appeared. She raised a triumphant two-thumbs-up as the crowd cheered. The plane catapulted forward on a rut-filled, grassy field for some fifty feet before lurching upward. Harriet was airborne.

She was off to a seamless start and things were progressing smoothly until a sudden gust of wind hit the plane from the left, causing the right wing to dip dangerously close to the ground. Harriet struggled to apply the opposite stick to warp the wing and pulled back on the elevator control. Slowly, the craft regained balance and Harriet rose to an altitude of approximately 150 feet at roughly 45 miles per hour. Bleriot-type planes were known to be awkward to control and Harriet called on her high degree of dexterity while she focused on the horizon to keep the plane level. As she turned, she continued to alternate her gaze between the horizon and ground markers that indicated her required turning points. This allowed her to execute the necessary flat skidding turns with the use of the rudder.

Another gust of wind hit the plane and, this time, the left wing fell to a dangerous tilt. Instinctively, Harriet applied full-force pressure on the stick. She knew she had to turn into the dropped wing or the plane could stall and then drop like a stone to the ground. Bleriot planes were also nose-heavy. Harriet realized all too well that the engine might quit, but for now, by its sound and the fine oily mist striking her goggles and face, she knew she was not in danger.

Harriet completed the remaining configurations without mishap, then circled the field and landed. She had successfully passed the first two parts of her examination. When flying Bleroit planes, it was necessary for pilots to land periodically to allow the engine to cool. The previous day, Harriet had landed and in her excitement, shut down the engine too soon. She would not make the same mistake twice. Today as she waited for the engine to cool, she focused on the final part of her exam. When she felt sufficient time had passed, Harriet climbed back into her plane. She noted her touchdown spot, then proceeded with her glide slope. As she neared six feet from the ground she pulled back on the lever, flared, and then began her descent. This time, Harriet did not miss her mark. The plane's wheels touched down at the precise location. Struggling to contain her excitement, she verbally counted off three seconds before turning off the switch that shut down the engine.

She had done it! Her monoplane had set down seven feet, nine inches from the mark. Not only had she achieved a successful landing, Harriet had also broken the previous record for test landings. A subsequent examination with a barograph (now known as an altimeter) determined that Harriet had also set a new record for flight altitude. She had flown fifty-eight feet higher than the previous record set—reaching 220 feet.

When a group of women emerged from the crowd to congratulate her, Harriet quipped, "Believe me, flying is much easier than voting." She was right. Women's fight for the right to vote would take another nine years. Harriet focused on maneuvering her way, smiling and waving, through the cheering crowd to the two aviation officials seated beside the flight line. She relished their support and her accomplishment. The crowd parted, then hushed, as she stood before the officials. "Well," she said evenly, "I guess I earned my license." The two men looked at each other, not pleased with what they were now forced to confirm. "Yes, we suppose you have," they replied in unison. Harriet's glorious smile shown through her face covered with grease and dirt. The crowd went wild (*New York Times*, 1911).

Although the *New York Times* covered the triumphant event, for some reason not one reporter from *Leslie's Weekly* was on hand to congratulate their popular staff member. The *Times* reported that on August 1, 1911, Harriet had become the first American woman to receive her pilot's license. She was, the article noted, the second woman in the world to achieve the goal, and the thirty-seventh person, male or female, to join the ranks of licensed flyers. Asked if aviation was dangerous, Harriet told reporters, "Yes, and so is swimming, if one tries to swim through Niagara. So is skating on thin ice. Bicycling, motoring, and many other activities in which we constantly indulge are perilous unless conditions are made safe. Over good ground, flying on a calm day, driving an aeroplane is as safe as driving an automobile in a crowded city; yet, with a clear-headed pilot, it need not be excessively dangerous" (New York Times, 1911).

During the early days of aviation, many were learning to fly, but most never bothered to earn a license. Only one woman had preceded Harriet—the Baroness de La Roche, of France, whose real name was Elise Raymonde Deroche. The self-styled baroness acquired license number thirty-six from the Internationale Aeronautics Federation in March 1910, at age twenty-four, just fifteen months prior to Harriet's accomplishment. Young and pretty, with a background surprisingly similar to Harriet's, the first female in the world to earn a pilot's license was described as a French lyrical artist and comedienne, which in the jargon of the day meant she, too, had been an "actress." She also wrote for magazines, penning one of her experiences for *Collier's* just two months after Harriet's tragic death. In "Flying in the Presence of the Czar," she described her participation in aviation exhibitions at Budapest and St. Petersburg, where the Tsar himself had praised her bravery and audacity. Baronesse de la Roche continued to participate in exhibitions throughout Europe until World War I interrupted her flying career. Shortly after the Great War ended, she returned to the air, but in 1919, at an aerodome outside Crotoy, she suffered a fatal crash. She was thirty-three years old.

Blanche Stuart Scott, an American ten years younger than Harriet, might have superseded Harriet in her accomplishment, but for some reason never pursued her pilot's license, even after receiving flying instruction from the famous Glenn Curtiss, whose aviation career Harriet had studied and admired for many years. Scott had made her own flying debut at an air meet in Fort Wayne, Indiana, in October 1910, as a member of the Curtiss Exhibition Team. Her flying prowess eventually earned her the nickname "tomboy of the air" (Harris, 1970). Later she became an accomplished stunt pilot known for flying upside down and performing death dives. From an altitude of 4,000 feet, Scott would suddenly drop almost to the earth, only to pull up abruptly, often a mere 200 feet and milliseconds from crashing onto the field. The crowds loved her daredevil antics.

Scott had been flying in the same air meet the day of Harriet's fatal crash and was deeply moved by the tragedy. She flew for five more years before finally retiring from exhibition flying in 1916, stating that she could no longer take the public's seemingly insatiable appetite for pilot injury and death. However, aviation remained her passion throughout her eighty-four years.

No one knows whether the Aero Club scoffed at the Baroness de la Roche for earning her pilot's license. However, the American officials who reluctantly issued Harriet's license were now faced with presiding over Matilde's test. Perhaps in retaliation for Harriet's success, they refused to test Matilde until Ferdinand de Muria, the male they had come to test in the first place, completed his exam. Harriet calmed her friend as they waited patiently on the sidelines while de Muria took off in another Moisant monoplane. Everything appeared to be going smoothly until it came time to land. Suddenly, de Muria overshot his mark, causing him to nosedive into the tail of the plane Matilde was to fly. Needless to say, de Muria did not earn his license that day and Matilde was forced to wait another two weeks while her aircraft was repaired. She earned her pilot's license fourteen days after Harriet.

Both women were exceptional flyers. Male skepticism inspired them even further. Matilde was often quoted as saying that women would eventually show men that they could fly and break neither the machine nor their necks in doing so. Even instructor Houpert admitted he had come to believe that women were the better pilots and a flying machine was safer in a woman's hands.

Male or female, it was difficult for most pilots to earn money flying. It was often a hand-to-mouth existence, even if one participated in the many air exhibitions in the US and abroad. A flyer could negotiate twenty to thirty-five percent of the net earnings of the event, but out of that would come mechanics' fees, aircraft transport costs, hangar rentals, fuel, and swag for those accompanying the entourage. Similar to today's groupies who tag along with rock stars and celebrities, these individuals catered to the needs and whims of these flying rock stars. Harriet had such followers wherever she went.

Two months after receiving her license, Harriet earned her first fee as a flyer, $1,500, at the Richmond County Fair on Staten Island. Her arrival was so anticipated that officials had to clear the landing field of the more than 20,000 people who had gathered to cheer her on. Harriet helped clear her takeoff path by driving her sporty yellow roadster ahead of the officials, like the grandmaster in the Macy's Day Parade.

Her flight course for the Richmond County meet led her across New York Bay and the busy Port of New York. She rose 2,000 feet before returning to Staten Island through clear skies and the light of a brilliant full moon. As she approached the field, Harriet waved a white handkerchief and swooped low as though she would skim the grandstand. The crowd waved and cheered. Before she could land, however, some overly enthusiastic spectators rushed onto the landing strip as she began her descent. She skimmed past her mark and was able to touch down a few feet beyond the crowd, but not before the craft bounced several times into the air, nearly ejecting her from the cockpit. To Harriet's great relief, the only damage to the plane was a few broken wires.

She was asked how she felt about being the first American pilot to fly at night. Despite the near tragedy that evening, she told reporters, "I was more interested in the beautiful view and how I was so tempted to just keep going until I reached New York City" (*New York Times*, 1912). She added that even with the chill of the night breeze, she was aware of being quite warm while in the air and attributed it to the great excitement she felt when hearing the roar of the crowd.

Harriet was becoming America's sweetheart. She received anonymous poetry from men and dozens of marriage proposals, along with hundreds of gifts that included everything from flowers to jewelry. Though most appreciative, she returned as many gifts as possible with a sincere thank-you along with a firm request not to continue the kindness. Harriet would do nothing to disparage her work as a reporter or her new goal of becoming America's most famous aviator, nor anything that would negate her character in the public's eye.

Harriet's charisma and prowess as a flyer made her a favorite at air shows throughout the country, so she had no trouble finding exhibitions welcoming her participation. Shortly after the Staten Island meet, she returned to Nassau Boulevard and the same field where she had earned her license to race France's leading woman pilot in 1911, Helene Dutrieu. Dutrieu was one of the few early aviators who enjoyed a long life as a pilot. After World War I, she became a journalist in France but continued to fly. She became the director of the women's section of the Aero Club of France a few years before her death in Paris in 1961, at age eighty-three. At the Nassau Boulevard exhibition in 1911, however, Dutrieu lost the cross-county race and the $600 prize money to Harriet Quimby.

Two weeks later, Harriet performed again, this time in an exhibition at the Trenton State Fair in New Jersey. Here she won another $1,500 purse and held the distinction of being not only the first American woman to earn her pilot's license, but the first licensed professional female aviator. Her reputation continued to grow and she and Matilde were star attractions of the Moisant flying team.

In fall 1911, Alfred Moisant contracted his troupe to perform at a festival planned in Mexico City to honor the country's new president, Francisco Madero. His team had been guaranteed $100,000 in purse money to participate in the inaugural ceremony. Harriet went by boat, continuing to file articles for *Leslie's* from her stateroom on the liner *Lamasa*. Matilde and other members of the group flew to the Mexican capital, while the team's six monoplanes, two biplanes, and the indispensable mechanics traveled by rail.

They were scheduled to tour Mexico from October through December, with each day-to-day experience providing fodder for Harriet's pen. Her editors at *Leslie's* knew sales potential when they saw it and encouraged her newfound second career, as long as she continued to write about her adventures in Mexico and, of course, flying in general. Every issue featuring an aviation article by Harriet sold out as soon as it hit the stands.

Unfortunately, political unrest led by rebel Emilio Zapata brought about a sudden change in plans for Alfred Moisant and his flyers. Harriet and the other troupe members barely escaped when rebels attacked the town where they were about to perform. Alfred had had enough. The group returned to the United States with Zapata and his men nipping at their heels, but not before Harriet, Matilde, and team members George Dycott and Charles Willard entertained thousands of spectators throughout the country. The Mexican press dubbed Harriet "the laughing girl" and praised her for her spirit and her beauty (*Leslie's Illustrated Weekly*, 1911).

Despite her love for flying, Matilde harbored a healthy fear of its potential dangers, particularly after her brother John's untimely death. She had had several serious accidents during her short career, as opposed to Harriet, who always managed to walk away from her airplane with a smile on her face and her aircraft unscathed.

After returning from Mexico, Matilde decided to quit flying. She considered thirteen her lucky number and decided March 13, 1912, would be her last exhibition. What was to be her farewell appearance in Wichita Falls, Texas, nearly turned out to be the last thing she ever did. As she circled the field and began her descent, she watched in horror as the crowd began to rush toward the landing strip. She panicked as she realized that she was about to kill someone, perhaps even herself. Her split-second decision was that if someone had to die, it would be her. She maneuvered the plane skyward about thirty feet, then descended even faster and with such force that the plane's gas tank exploded, engulfing the wooden fuselage in flames. The ground crew worked desperately to drag her from the intense flames. Miraculously, her actions had made the crowd scatter so no one was injured, but Matilde was badly burned.

That was the last time Matilde took to the air. "The earth is bound to get us after a while," she said, "so I shall give up flying before I follow my brother" (Oakes, 1978). She broke this promise to herself only once. At the outbreak of World War I, she volunteered to fly overseas as part of General Pershing's expeditionary force. The United States government turned down her request. "Though we appreciate your interest," government officials wrote her, "it is not the intention of the United States to take women into the actual dangers of the war zone unless the need becomes imperative" (Oakes, 1978). It would be another sixty years before the US military seriously considered admitting women pilots to the armed forces, and twenty years beyond that before the government considered the issue of women pilots in combat. Matilde became a Red Cross nurse stationed in France, where she remained until the end of the war. She and Harriet never flew together again, but she would always remain one of Harriet's biggest fans.

By 1912, Harriet was recognized as one of the most skilled pilots of the time and the highest-profile female flyer in America. But some people still doubted her ability. It was for this reason that an idea she hatched during her Mexico tour was about to become a reality. Harriet was upping the stakes once again on her quest for the next adventure.

"The time is coming when we shall find the means of transportation by bird-like flights as safe and satisfactory as transportation by steamship or locomotive and with still greater speed. This is not to be accomplished by racing or doing circus tricks in the air at aviation meets." —Harriet Quimby

CHANNEL MARKER

Harriet's next goal was to be the first woman to fly across the English Channel. Fearing one of her European counterparts would accomplish the feat before her, she kept her plans under wraps. Only a few of her trusted advisors, including her editors at *Leslie's Weekly*, knew the reason she journeyed to England in March of 1912 with A. Leo Stevens. He had been at dinner the evening Harriet talked John and Alfred Moisant into admitting her to their flight school and was Harriet's manager and rumored lover. He was an old hand in the fledgling world of aviation. In 1912 he owned one of the most successful balloon foundries in the country, producing spherical balloons for customers worldwide. He had been issued balloon license number 2 from the Aero Club, and in his later years became one of the first civilian inspectors of aircraft for the United States Army.

Harriet also carried to England a letter of introduction to Louis Bleriot himself. Before her scheduled trip, the noted airplane designer had sent Bernard Alfieri, a photographer and Bleriot representative, to meet Harriet in New York City and discuss her plans. At that meeting, Harriet hoped to convince Alfieri that flying a Bleriot plane across the English Channel would boost the aircraft's sales in this country. Of course, she was also interested in increasing her status in American aviation and elevating her reputation as the top female flyer in aviation history.

Alfieri must have agreed. Harriet and Stevens departed for England aboard the SS *Amerika* and went directly to the *London Daily Mirror* headquarters. *Leslie's* had already quietly agreed to be her American sponsor once the flight was arranged. Harriet understood a newspaper's nose for news and thought that the *Mirror* would agree to an exclusive story in exchange for European sponsorship.

At first shocked that a woman would attempt such a dangerous endeavor, the *Mirror* editors understood that a woman attempting such a venture, especially someone from "the colonies," would make interesting reading. Besides, they reasoned, Americans were always doing strange things. They agreed to sponsor Harriet with the "handsome inducement" of $5,000 for the exclusive European rights to her story. *Leslie's Illustrated Weekly* would still hold exclusive US rights.

Harriet and Stevens then sailed across the channel to meet with Bleriot himself and inquire about purchasing an aircraft for her flight. At his factory in Calais, France, Bleriot showed the two his new seventy-horsepower monoplane. Harriet knew its speed and ease of maneuverability was what she needed for the crossing. Her plan was to use the plane to fly over the English Channel and then take it back to the United States. She was disappointed to learn that the plane she wanted would not be ready for several weeks. This was precious time lost when someone else might attempt to fly the English Channel. Harriet convinced Bleriot to at least sell her the seventy-horsepower monoplane and lend her a fifty-horsepower model for the channel crossing.

No one knew better than he the danger of this feat. After developing the first practical head lamp for cars, Bleriot had used the profits to finance his love of flying and to build aircraft. In 1909, he became world-famous for making the first flight across the English Channel. Bleriot knew of Harriet's reputation as a skilled flyer, but he also understood the risk of losing one of his aircraft at sea. He was a businessman first and foremost. She paid a deposit on the seventy-horsepower plane and Stevens signed a promissory note agreeing to pay for the plane if Harriet's flight across the channel was not successful.

Despite her attempts at secrecy, Harriet's activities were leaked to other European newspapers. Much to her dismay, another European aviator, Gustav Hamel, stole some of Harriet's thunder by flying a Mrs. Eleanor Trehawke Davies across the English Channel several days before Harriet's venture. True, she had been a passenger, but now she was technically the first female to fly over the English Channel. As a result, Harriet lost monetary support from several backers at the *Mirror*, but that was the least of her worries.

Harriet had never flown an authentic Bleriot monoplane and wanted to try out the machine in an environment where she might draw little attention. Bleriot's hangar was located at Hardelot and he suggested she do some trial runs there. The small resort town was far from bustling city crowds and the press.

As she reported later, the trip to Hardelot, where Bleriot also had a seaside home, was not pleasant. The main route from Paris to the town was through Boulogne. When she arrived there after enduring a dusty two-hour journey, it was impossible to find a cab. Her only other option was to board a derelict-looking tram car. Even worse, the upcoming Easter holiday made the crowds intolerable. When she finally reached her destination, she was more than ready to get to the hotel Bleriot had recommended. To her dismay, "The fine hotel," Harriet wrote later, "was closed and dark" (*New York Times*, 1912).

With halting French, Harriet was able to explain her predicament to someone, who then directed her to a small cottage in the middle of town. With her limited French and her hosts' faltering English, she successfully communicated her need for lodging. Grateful as she was, Harriet was not used to the provincialism of this rural town. It would serve its purpose, she told herself, and set her sights on flying the English Channel.

Gale-force winds kept Harriet from testing the plane for several days. During her stay, an English family in Hardelot heard of the young American and sent an automobile and invitation to lunch at their nearby home. Harriet readily agreed, but she knew she had to get back to England soon before word of her anticipated flight leaked to the public. She finally was able to complete her tests, but before departing Harriet journeyed to the site where Bleriot had completed the first channel crossing three years earlier. She noted the fine granite marker celebrating his successful flight. Observing that the

Dover cliffs loomed ominously high, she decided to chart her flight in reverse of Bleriot's. She would fly from England to France to avoid the daunting cliffs of Dover. By doing so, she would map her course in the same direction as her mentor, John Moisant, the first American to achieve the flight across the channel, the same year as Bleriot.

The Bleriot aircraft, though primitive by today's standards, served as the foundation for aeronautical development. Planes still trace their roots to the Bleriot model. Louis Bleriot created the enclosed fuselage, the engine placement in front of the pilot's seat, and rudder and rear elevator placement on the craft's stabilizer. Bleriot and Curtiss aircraft were the two most copied designs of their day. John Moisant was one of the more successful copiers.

Although the Bleriot monoplane was rather fragile and spindly, its many advantages made it Harriet's first choice. It was light and simple to maintain, and easy to disassemble and set up for flight. This was an important feature to an exhibition pilot. The Bleriot aircraft required just thirty minutes prep time, compared to other planes that required as many as eight hours to prepare for flight. The Bleriot plane air-cooled and a Gnome rotary engine provided another edge in its reliability and low weight per horsepower. The Gnome engine weighed approximately 580 pounds, compared to biplane engines weighing up to 985 pounds. In addition, Bleriot flying machines were carefully crafted with wood and canvas held together with wire and glue. Before each flight, fuselage alignment, wheels, tires, wiring, and all surfaces were subjected to inspection. Well-trained professionals identified any problems and were prepared to eliminate them on the spot.

Harriet had secretly arranged for her plane to be shipped to Dover for the flight. The morning of April 14 dawned brilliantly sunny and clear. Her friends Linda Arvidson Griffith and Carrie Vanderbilt had flown to England to support her. Harriet joined them at the aerodome in Dover, along with Monsieur Norbert Chereau, manager of Bleriot's London office, and his wife Madame Chereau. Gustav Hamel had come to the field as well. The seasoned British pilot knew Harriet had never flown over water or used a compass, and he wanted to show her how to use it. Harriet resisted, but Hamel insisted she carry it with her. Many fliers had lost their lives trying to make the crossing, and he reminded her that if she should fly even five miles off course, she might disappear into the frigid channel. Tragically, not long thereafter, Hamel would meet that very fate. Hamel tested Harriet's plane. He even offered to fly the mission for her—dressed in disguise. Harriet politely declined, but begrudgingly agreed to carry the compass.

Successful flights from the Dover aerodome demanded still air, which was the prevailing condition that day. Harriet could see Calais dimly outlined twenty-two miles across the channel. Predictions for the coming week forecast high winds and heavy rain that would make her mission impossible. There was just one problem that the crowd assembled that morning could not have been aware of. It was generally known in the United States that Harriet was highly superstitious and no one gave much thought to her use of good-luck charms and symbolic trinkets. What people did not know was that Harriet did not fly on Sundays. She had promised her mother that she would not fly on the Sabbath for any reason. However, April 14, the perfect weather day for her record-breaking English Channel crossing, was a Sunday. Despite her eagerness to achieve her goal, Harriet announced to the crowd that she would not fly on this day. She would wait and take her chances later in the week.

Harriet remained cheerful. Only her friends and Leo Stevens stayed with her after the ground crew and the disappointed onlookers departed. Perhaps it would be best for Harriet to wait for another day, they agreed. Certainly, none would question her decision. They drove back to the hotel, chatting as though just returning from a pleasant Sunday afternoon outing. The flight was not mentioned and Harriet cheerily assured them that tomorrow was another day.

As predicted, Monday swept in thick clouds, gusting winds, and heavy rain. Harriet and her ground crew huddled inside the damp hangar at the aerodome waiting for the weather to clear. Reporters gathered, as did some die-hard spectators, but as the day progressed it became clear that not even a crazy person would attempt such a feat in this weather. "All things come to those who wait," Harriet told them (*New York Times*, 1912). She did not have to wait much longer to make history.

By Tuesday, April 16, the rain stopped and the winds subsided, though some patchy fog remained. Harriet, Arvidson, Vanderbilt, and Stevens climbed into Hamel's automobile at 3:30 that morning. Harriet noted the air was chilly, but there was no wind. In fact, she reported later, there was "scarcely a breath of air at all" (*New York Times*, 1912). She ordered Hamel to hurry, for she anticipated that the wind would rise after the sun came up. Once at the field, the group worked together to push the monoplane out of the hangar, then peered at the horizon for the first light of day. The sky was clear above her, but Harriet could see in the distance that the French coast was obscured by a moving wall of mist. She could wait no longer.

Harriet climbed into the plane. In addition to the compass, Hamel provided Harriet with a hot water bottle to place on her lap. At first she refused the compass, saying that she had never needed one (not admitting that she had no idea how to use it). Always cautious, Harriet explained that she did not want the slightest bit of added weight that could hinder the aircraft. Hamel insisted, however, reminding Harriet that she would be flying 6,000 feet above sea level through unpredictable skies. She reluctantly relented.

She saw the crowd waving handkerchiefs as her plane pushed off, but could not hear their cheers of encouragement above the engine roaring at 1,200 rpms as she began her ascent. It was 5:30 a.m.

Later, in an article for *Leslie's*, Harriet wrote, "On takeoff, I saw at once that I had only to rise in my machine, fix my eyes on Dover Castle, fly over it directly to the French coast. It seemed so easy" (*Leslie's Illustrated Weekly*, 1912). In the same article, she reported that she was relieved to feel so at ease, or otherwise she may have been more hesitant about flying into the fog using only a compass that was unfamiliar to her. She was all too aware of the menacing North Sea ready to receive her if she drifted off course. What she did not know was that on the same day an English navigator named D. Leslie Allen had attempted a flight over the Irish Channel from London to Dublin and had lost course, plunging into the water. His body was never recovered.

As she flew, Harriet climbed steadily to 1,500 feet. She could still see Dover Castle through a veil of mist, but the tugboat of reporters sent from the *Mirror* to follow her course was barely discernible. Suddenly a wave of heavy fog engulfed her. It became so thick, so rapidly, she could no longer make out the water or coastline below. The thin ribbon of black smoke emitted from the tugboat guided her for a time, but she soon outpaced it. The fog grew thicker as she climbed. She knew the spectators were panicked as they watched the monoplane dissolve into the mist.

Harriet wore her watch, which at least helped her gauge how far she had flown. She began to climb again, desperately searching for a hole through the fog that cocooned her. Though flying now at an altitude above 6,000 feet, Harriet reported later that she was not cold. "The excitement, I guess, stimulated me," she reported.

Harriet determinedly tried using the compass. Besides her watch, it was her only possible frame of reference. The intense concentration exhausted her and began to take their toll on her senses. She listened intently for the engine's hum, knowing all too well that if it should quit, she would never survive a crash-landing into the cold waters of the English Channel.

Harriet estimated that she had been in the air for approximately twenty-two minutes. She decided it was time to descend, or at least attempt to do so. As she maneuvered her plane into position, the Bleriot suddenly tilted to a steep angle that caused the gasoline to flood the engine. This was a major flaw in the Bleriot design and was responsible for several pilots' demise. As the plane began to backfire, Harriet maintained control of the aircraft and considered her options. "I decided to pancake into the water to a floating position," she reported in a subsequent *Leslie's* article, "for I knew there was a balloon-like flotation device running the length of the fuselage" (*Leslie's Illustrated Weekly*, 1912). As she also knew, however, this strategy would not work for long. Fortunately, the gasoline burned away in short order and the engine returned to its previous hum.

Harriet continued her descent, estimating and hoping that she would be close to the French coast when she emerged from the fog. As the plane moved into brilliant sunlight, Harriet's gaze met a thin line of white sand outlining the green grass of the French coast. Her goal of being the first American woman to fly solo across the English Channel had been accomplished in one hour and nine minutes.

Flying a short distance inland, Harriet found a place to land. She was glad to be on the ground, but she was not sure she had reached Calais. As she gathered her bearings, the silence erupted as fishermen, women, and children chatting rapidly in French emerged from the countryside and gathered around her. She had touched down in Hardelot, the same village where she had traveled to borrow the Bleriot. She knew her friends, crew, and supporters were waiting for her in Calais. In her limited French, she asked a fisher boy to take a message to the nearest telegraph office in Hardelot and send word to Calais that she had arrived safely. "The people could not have been more helpful or friendly," Harriet wrote. "They made me understand that my airplane should be moved so it would not be carried away with the rising tide. They handled my aircraft most gently, and I was grateful for that" (*Leslie's Illustrated Weekly*, 1912).

One particular act of kindness touched Harriet deeply, and she spoke of it often after returning to the United States. Soon after she had landed, one of the fisher women insisted on serving Harriet a welcoming cup of steaming hot tea with a large serving of bread and cheese. She described the cup as six times larger than any teacup she had ever seen, and its design as so charming and quaint that she could not conceal her admiration. The villager insisted that Harriet keep it as a remembrance of her achievement. "No cup I ever won or ever shall win as an aero trophy will be prized more than this one," Harriet told the woman (*Leslie's Illustrated Weekly*, 1912).

Soon *Mirror* reporters were on the scene; much to Harriet's great embarrassment, a crowd of people lifted her to their shoulders and paraded her through the village streets to waving well-wishers. Her dream had come true. She envisioned headlines around the world proclaiming "America's Darling Premier Female Pilot Conquers English Channel." That might have been the case, but for an incomprehensible tragedy that had occurred only forty-eight hours before Harriet's record flight. On April 14, in the deep waters of the North Atlantic Ocean, the "unsinkable" White Star liner *Titanic* had struck an iceberg and sunk into the frigid waves, claiming the lives of 1,573 passengers. The SS *Carpathia* had not yet reached the site to report on the devastation at the time Harriet lifted her monoplane toward the cliffs of Dover.

As Harriet basked in the celebration of her success, no one was yet aware of the tragedy. She was driven back to Calais for the quick train ride to Paris and arrived that evening "quite exhausted, but deliriously happy," she told her readers. Harriet was surely unprepared for the startling lack of attention she received. Had she not been superstitious and had flown on Sunday, she might have at least shared headlines with the ill-fated ship before the extent of the disaster was known. As it was, the tragedy dominated newspaper coverage worldwide for weeks. The *New York Times*, one of Harriet's staunchest supporters besides her own employer, relegated her success to page fifteen, after prominently reporting on her every move for over a year. Even the *London Daily Mirror* buried the story in its advertisements for theater and fashion.

The *New York Times* acknowledgment of her feat was not only several weeks late, but insulting. An editorial entitled "Exultation Not In Order" assured readers that Miss Quimby's achievement did not pass unnoticed, but somewhat apologetically noted that the public's attention to the *Titanic* tragedy was more newsworthy than another flight over the English Channel. The reporter reminded readers that many men had crossed the channel and that women would not want to recognize her achievement as "great for women." The article concluded that something done the first time is one thing; after the seventh or eighth time, it becomes less impressive and does not prove that women and men are equal. The writer advised feminists to refrain from celebrating a relatively minor achievement. Harriet was astounded and disappointed.

Never one to let an anonymous pen stifle her defense, Harriet responded in an article for *Leslie's*. "I wish my views on the subject of feminism could be understood," she wrote. "It is not a fad, and I did not want to be the first American woman to fly just to make myself conspicuous. I am just living my life, going after goals, and continuing to evolve" (*Leslie's Illustrated Weekly*, 1912).

After that April morning in 1912, aviation would become a more complex and integral part of the global community. It is hard to fully appreciate the extreme danger Harriet Quimby faced in her brief, twenty-two-mile channel flight. Just nine years earlier, the Wright brothers had achieved the first powered flight. Bleriot's monoplane had the dubious reputation as the trickiest aircraft the French designer had yet produced.

Several flyers before Harriet's flight had lost their lives. So primitive was flight at that time that one did not fly in fog, rain, or clouds, at night, or in more than a five-mile-per-hour wind. There were no parachutes, no guidance equipment to speak of, no radio or navigational charts to follow. Moving over a body of water with no sight of land was perilous at best.

When Harriet flew the channel, fog and rain obscured most of her journey. She flew a plane that warped its wings in order to bank and required equal amounts of gasoline, prayer, and luck. It took an enormous amount of courage, skill, and self-confidence for anyone, male or female, to attempt such a venture. Harriet played down her achievement, writing, "The trip was as easy as sitting at home in an armchair. I never had any doubt of my success, and any woman with sufficient self-confidence and cool head could fly across the English Channel as easily as I" (*Leslie's Illustrated Weekly*, 1912). However, in subsequent articles, she could not resist the temptation to chide skeptics, writing "I believe women are more fearless than men or at least I have more requests for flight trips now from them. Many women inquire as to how to fly for sport, or even as an occupation, which is a fine thought" (*Leslie's Illustrated Weekly*, 1912). She jokingly told friends she would make flying a career if she did not enjoy exhibitions and writing so much.

Harriet did acknowledge that the cost of flying, rather than being female, prevented many women from flying. She predicted that as soon as the price of lessons and the cost of operating a machine decreased so that the average person could participate, it would become a popular pastime for women. Unfortunately, over 100 years later, the major impediment to female pilots is still largely economic, along with a lack of female mentors and support systems to encourage women to enter aviation as a profession or for recreation (Patterson, 2007).

FASHIONABLE FLYER

Appearing feminine and fashionable was always important to Harriet, and she knew that women looked to her for the latest fashion trends. So as her air show appearances increased, she was dismayed when critics commented on her unflattering flight attire. It was true. Harriet did piece together her flight outfits using men's clothing.

For centuries, society severely restricted women's fashion, strapping them into corsets that contorted the female frame into an exaggerated hourglass shape. Dresses laden with lace, ruffles, and frills hindered sudden movement, while women's heads balanced wide-brimmed hats adorned with fruit, flowers, and other assorted bobbles plundered from the animal kingdom. Among the most abused species were wrens, thrushes, ostriches, and the poor egret—the latter, easily caught while tending its young, reigned as the hat ornament of choice in Harriet's day.

Outraged, Harriet had urged her *Leslie's* readers to write their congressmen and senators, telling them if something is not done, and done quickly, society would be smarting under the disgrace of having looked on calmly while American birds and wildlife were gradually annihilated. The government eventually heard the pleas of Harriet and others. Laws were passed to end the killing of birds with the exception of the flamingo and passenger pigeon.

But now, what a fashionable aviatrix should wear become a pressing issue for Harriet and other style-conscious women flyers. Simply donning men's pants or trouserettes, as polite society called them, might have been practical, but in a country emerging from the Victorian era, it was seen as immoral. In 1911, a popular clergyman in Hartford, Connecticut, delivered a scathing Sunday sermon about the vulgarity of costumes worn by women of the day. He told his congregation that the masters of fashion seemed to be preparing women to take their place with men by copying elements of men's attire. Men everywhere, he said, were bemoaning the loss of the old-time womanly sweetness, modesty, and virtue they admired. He was not alone in his opinion.

Some women improvised by wearing trousers with rows of buttons on the inside that, when unbuttoned, converted to a chic ankle-length skirt. Others "hobbled" their skirts by tying them just below the knees, which was awkward and uncomfortable. For several years, the accepted flight attire for women was a modest two-piece outfit consisting of a blouse, wide-legged tweed knickers or riding pants, high-top boots, and a soft fabric helmet with goggles.

Harriet decided to take matters into her own hands. In "How A Woman Learns to Fly" (*Leslie's Weekly*, May 25, 1911), she wrote, "If a woman wants to fly she must, of course, abandon skirts." In early exhibitions she had worn a long scarf that trailed behind her in a wisp of purple haze. Now she drew on her modeling experience and innate femininity to refine what news accounts referred to as the drab, cumbersome, bulky sweaters and trouserettes and uncomfortable harem-type pants worn by fellow flyers Helen Dutrieu, the Baroness de la Roche, and Blanche Scott.

Harriet learned of a Fifth Avenue shop advertising ready-made driving clothes and flying attire for women. Never one to jeopardize her individuality by selecting an outfit off the rack, Harriet approached Alexander Green, president of the American Tailors Association headquartered in New York City. She shared her vision for clothing that would be both feminine and functional. Green sensed her place in destiny and desire to introduce a unique flying costume others would emulate. He was aware of Harriet's reputation for style and penchant for publicity and photo-ops. He studied her choice of dresses with flattering sailor collars that spread across her shoulders, drawing attention upward to frame her lovely face. Overhung bonnets, antique trinkets such as basilisks, amulets, and scarabs, and any variation of the color purple complemented her unique individuality. "It is a style I find comfortable and attractive," Harriet often said (*Good Housekeeping*, 1912). It did not take long for the talented designer to create a flying suit that would set a precedent for aviation fashion for women not only in the United States, but the world. Who better than Harriet Quimby to set the standard?

Green's creation was extraordinary for 1911: a one-piece costume with full knickers designed to skim just below the knee. Although rayon had been invented in 1910, Green's fashion was made of wool-backed satin. This fabric presented the appearance of heavy satin, but with an exquisitely lustrous crepe-like finish that billowed like silk with the wearer's every movement. *Vogue* described the "new silks" as made of a lustrous satin weave that does not float away, but rather, strengthened by the wool-like satin crepe, holds its drape in a flattering way (*Good Housekeeping*, 1912). The head gear resembled a monk's hood that lay shawl-like across the shoulders when not covering the head (patterned after Harriet's love of the sailor collar). Small swatches of black net stitched on both sides of the hood served to protect the ears while permitting the flyer to listen for the aircraft's familiar grunts and groans. High-laced black kid boots replaced the cumbersome boots. Updated accessories included elbow-length, gauntlet-style driving gloves, flying goggles, and a long leather coat designed for cold weather. The costume was a variation of her favorite color, purple. She loved this new fashion statement, telling Green that it was fashionable, yet functional: an ingenious combination that allowed its wearer to easily convert the knickerbockers to a conventional walking skirt.

AVIATION ADVOCACY

Reporters continued to hound her with questions about why a beautiful and successful journalist would not just be content with getting married and raising a family. They did not understand why she wanted more. Harriet, perhaps more clearly than most people, including fellow pilots, recognized the potential aviation offered as a productive and lucrative industry. She saw flying as a future source of employment for women. "The time is coming," she wrote, "when we shall find the means of transportation by bird-like flights as safe and satisfactory as transportation by steamship or locomotive *and* with still greater speed" (*Leslie's Weekly*, 1911).

Many decided that Harriet must be some type of radical feminist attempting to raise America's consciousness about women's rights. Reporters suggested she name her airplane Pankhurst for the leading English suffragette Mrs. Emmeline Pankhurst, who had come to the United States in 1906 to heighten public awareness of women's rights, or Catt, after the American feminist Carrie Chapman Catt. Harriet felt that these women used unflattering and unladylike ways to make their point, including disrupting public meetings and destroying public property. Instead, Harriet named her plane *Genevieve*, the patron saint of French pilots.

Even the question of what to call a female flyer posed a problem in the early days of aviation. Some used the word aviatrix, others air woman; still others suggested lumping male and female pilots under one label: aeronauts. Many, especially journalists, agreed that establishing a glossary of terms for the rapidly growing field of aeronautics was necessary. Newspapers settled on the neutral term "aviator" when reporting on pilots of either gender. Amazingly, the public did not seem ready for such a unisex term, and aviatrix was used to describe female flyers until the mid-1990s.

In addition to the issue of women taking to the air, safety continued to be a major debate. The new achievements recorded almost daily were offset by fatalities of would-be record-seekers. In a 1911 article for *Leslie's* entitled "The Dangers of Flying and How to Avoid Them," Harriet explained, "The aviator should be thinking more of his or her safety and less of public acclaim. This also encourages promoters of meets to have greater regard for the lives of flyers, rather than wanting to startle the public with perilous performance of stunts." In the article she chided the "male ego" and greed of exhibition coordinators. She reported that she had once received an invitation from a Chicago group for an event boasting a draw of $250,000, but, in fact, each aviator would receive only $1,000 as their share of the cut. "We would risk our lives and damage to our aircraft for a compensation that would barely cover expenses, which seemed highly unsportsmanlike to me," she wrote, adding that "for those really interested in aerial navigation for the benefit of the future, dangerous 'spiraling down' or 'banking' must come to be recognized as not only the lack of entertainment, but downright foolhardy. Only when this fancy flying has calmed down will the dangers of the air be diminished."

She reported that she declined the invitation despite her deeply held belief that when called to fly, pilots should do so no matter how they felt. "Not to do so," she concluded, "earned one the reputation for being what is known as a 'groundhog,' or one who has lost the nerve to fly."

AGE OF INNOCENCE

Despite her popularity, Harriet remained a mystery even to those who knew her well. An intensely private person, she liked this aura of mystique separating her from her ever-growing fan base. It suited her quirks and superstitious nature. Refusing to fly on Sundays, her odd-looking lucky jewelry that became part of her everyday attire, and her obsession with the odd amulets she collected on round-the-world junkets had become a trademark. Some of these trinkets were described as downright ugly and atypical of the art deco style popular at the time. One treasure was the Ganesha, a multi-limbed East Indian idol made from solid brass that many believed brought successful travels and general good luck.

> *"He was such a cute little fellow and I never had a bit of trouble in the air after I got him in England."*—Harriet Quimby

As the story goes, Harriet had a daily custom of scanning publications while sipping her morning tea. One morning in England, as she awaited favorable weather conditions for her channel crossing, several stories in the *London Daily Mirror* caught her eye. The famed American aviator, Calbraith Perry "Cal" Rodgers, had been killed in California while flying a Wright biplane. A dance called the Sherlockinette, named for the popular author Arthur Conan Doyle, was all the rage in London. Most intriguing to Harriet was a small item in "Letters to the Editor" responding to an article that had been featured in the *Mirror* several weeks earlier. *Mirror* editor Alexander Kenealy had solicited and received what were believed to be good luck oddities. Among them was a brass Ganesha from a French pilot claiming the talisman had brought him terrible misfortune. The flyer had requested that someone destroy the object for him, for he was afraid that destroying it himself would attract additional trouble. The *Mirror* sought a volunteer to fulfill the pilot's wish. Unbeknownst to Harriet, this was another publicity stunt by Kenealy, fondly referred to as "Tubby" by coworkers. He regularly called for the collection of amulets, idols, and other good (or bad) luck charms, some of which would be featured in a story. Harriet read that only one person had responded—an agent who wanted her young actress client to destroy the Ganesha as a publicity stunt. The actress declined, fearing her career would be ruined.

Despite her own superstitious nature, Harriet seized the opportunity for publicity. She went to the *Mirror* office to meet Kenealy and selected the Ganesha as her new good-luck souvenir. She had done her homework and learned that in the Buddhist tradition, Ganesha was considered the "remover of all obstacles" and the god of success (Brown, 1991). Photographs from her historic English Channel crossing show Harriet clutching her new talisman in her hand as she prepared for flight. "He was such a cute little fellow, and I never had a bit of trouble with him since obtaining him in England," she wrote in *Leslie's Weekly* on her return to the United States. Three months later, Harriet was gone. The "lucky" Ganesha was found buried in the mud beneath her body at the crash site.

When she read of Cal Rodgers' death in the *Mirror* before her first channel crossing, Harriet could not have known how their fates would intertwine. Like Harriet, Calbraith Perry Rodgers was single-minded and did not give up until his goal was achieved. He was the grandson of Commodore Calbraith Perry, whose "gunboat diplomacy" opened Japan to the West in 1854. In 1911, the thirty-two-year-old, cigar-smoking, flamboyant pilot responded to William Randolph Hearst's offer of $50,000 to be the first man to make a transcontinental flight in thirty days or less. He had attended the Wright Brothers flying school and, always a quick study, completed his training in a record ninety minutes. The plane he flew for Hearst's challenge was similar to the original Wright flyer the brothers had used on their first flight in Kitty Hawk in 1903. A thirty-five-horsepower, single speed, four-cylinder engine with a fifteen-gallon gas tank, it could remain in the air for approximately three and a half hours.

Rodgers secured his own sponsorship for the journey from the Armour Meat Packing Company headquartered in Chicago, in return for helping to promote the company's new grape-flavored soft drink Vin Fiz. Before takeoff, the airplane was christened with a bottle of the drink and its name was prominently displayed in purple across the aircraft's wings and tail. As Rodgers flew over the major cities along his cross-country route, people gazed skyward to see the Vin Fiz logo passing by. It was the birth of aerial advertising in this country.

Rodgers took off from Sheepshead Bay, Long Island, on September 17, 1911, and landed in Pasadena, California, nearly three months later. His flight was not smooth. Less than a day out of Sheepshead, he wrecked the aircraft and had to completely rebuild it, delaying his journey five days. This was only the first of five mishaps, two engine explosions, and dozens of minor incidents. In addition to mechanical problems, he was plagued with navigational errors. The *Vin Fiz* carried no navigational instruments, not even a compass. Rodgers was forced to "follow the line," navigating from town to town by following the railroad tracks. If he chose the wrong track, he would travel for miles before realizing how far off course he had gone (*Airport Journal*, 2011).

Nonetheless, he kept going. When he finally reached Long Beach, California, eighty-four days after departing Sheepshead, a crowd of 50,000 people cheered as the *Vin Fiz* touched down in the Pacific surf. Rodgers had flown 4,321 miles in eighty-two hours flying time, at an average speed of fifty-two mph. Unfortunately, he did not earn Hearst's $50,000 prize money since the crossing took him well over thirty days. Rodgers settled for $20,000 from the Armour Company for spreading the word about Vin Fiz. Sadly, Rodgers died less than a year later. During a routine flight, he swerved to miss a flock of sea gulls, hit one, and plunged into the surf just 500 feet from his triumphant landing five months earlier. The engine broke loose on impact, striking Rogers in the head and breaking his neck. A reconstructed *Vin Fiz* is now on display at the Smithsonian Air and Space Museum in Washington, DC.

Three months after Rodgers' fatal crash, the Armour Company asked Harriet to become its new spokesperson. It was an ingenious strategy, as by this time Harriet was known for her striking purple flying outfits and would complement print ads for the popular grape soda. In April 1912, Harriet posed for the famous poster that promoted Vin Fiz across the country and became the first female symbol for a brand in a national advertising campaign.

Harriet used Rodgers' death to continue her plea for safety improvements in aviation. She wrote, "The invention of the biplane, which is simply a box kite properly balanced and equipped with steering planes and a motor, has done much toward progress in air navigation. But the biplane is not a bird, nor does it fly like a bird. Everyone who has seen the monoplane, with its long and narrow body and outstretched wings, will agree" (*Leslie's Illustrated Weekly*, 1911).

Harriet believed that the monoplane best represented a bird in flight. What the monoplane had done to further the science of flying, she wrote, was being proven every day by flyers making 1,000-mile flights without mishap. She was quick to add that the great number of fatalities could not be attributed solely to the imperfections of the flying machine. "In nearly every case," she wrote, "the fatality was shown to be the reckless flying of the pilot" (*Leslie's Illustrated Weekly*, 1911).

"There is nothing to fear if one is careful. Only a cautious person should fly. I never mount my machine until I check every wire and screw. I have never had an accident in the air. It may be luck, but it is also to the care of a good mechanic." —Harriet Quimby

By 1912, Harriet was still the lone voice looking out for women in a male-dominated arena. She was concerned that one aeronautics manufacturer had offered flying lessons to women if, in return, they would serve as test pilots for their aircraft. Harriet adamantly opposed such a plan, writing in her column, "A skilled flyer would be a good advertisement for a manufacturer, but a highly dangerous proposition for a man, or woman, just beginning to fly" (*Leslie's Illustrated Weekly*, 1911).

She noted that some men in Europe attempted such work, but only a few very good flyers had succeeded without injury or death.

The status of women in journalism, too, continued to inch along at a snail's pace. When she entered the profession, there were few women journalists of note. This, despite the fact that the first newspaper in the world, *The Daily Courant*, was founded by a woman, Elizabeth Mallet, more than 200 years earlier. Harriet was pleased that more women were writing and seeking admission to prestigious schools to achieve higher-paying jobs. However, they were met with strong opposition from men in the profession.

Harriet encountered at least one powerful male who joined her quest to give women an equal chance to pursue whatever area of endeavor they might choose. Dr. James M. Lee, director of New York University's journalism school, published a rebuttal to opponents seeking to bar females from entering the Pulitzer School of Journalism at Columbia University. The parallels were clear to Harriet, who believed that Professor Lee's comments also applied to women in aviation. "The question," wrote Professor Lee, "is not whether women should go into journalism, they have already made strides into the field. The real question is whether women will be given an honest deal once admitted. Even if states object to giving voting rights to women, it does not mean they should object to allowing women journalism students to thrive. The public and publications alike should not be so much interested in the sex of a writer as they are in securing the best work for their audience. Give women a chance!" (Holden, 1993). A rally call, Harriet reported in *Leslie's*, she could not have proclaimed better herself.

BOSTON AIR MEET

One of the biggest air exhibitions in July 1912 was the Boston Air Meet at Squantum, Massachusetts, near Quincy. This event attracted the biggest names in aviation, but this year Harriet Quimby was unquestionably the main draw. Stevens had negotiated a reported fee of $100,000 for his client's participation. During the week-long event, Harriet would pilot the new two-seater Bleriot XI seventy-horsepower monoplane she had purchased in England. Louis Bleriot himself had delivered the state-of-the-art aircraft to the United States for Harriet to fly in this meet, which was expected to draw thousands. Publicity posters announced "Come See America's Greats" and "Don't Miss the Queen of the Channel Crossing Miss Harriet Quimby." It was the kind of publicity Harriet had expected when she made her historic flight two months earlier.

The Boston Light Air Meet was to be Harriet's farewell exhibition. She had announced plans to write a novel, something she had placed on hold many years ago until she was professionally and financially secure. The meet would take place at Harvard Field on Squantum Bay and promised to be a revenue gold mine for promoter William Willard. Stevens did not have to convince Willard of Harriet's drawing power. Like so many other men who crossed her path, Willard was smitten. In a press interview before the Boston meet, he told reporters that she was the prettiest girl he had ever seen. "She had the most beautiful blue eyes—yes, what eyes she had! She was tall and willowy, with silky dark hair and when she wore her long cape over her satin plum-colored flying suit, well, she was a real head turner (*Leslie's Illustrated Weekly*, 1912).

Harriet's new high-powered, two-passenger machine was originally designed for military use. When Harriet went to claim the plane upon its arrival from France, customs officials had no idea how to classify the aircraft and referred her to legal counsel. Some wanted to call it a "phantom horse" and pretend they did not see it arrive on US shores. After considerable argument as to how to identify Bleriot's latest airplane, officials settled on the customs category reserved for polo ponies, with the added footnote: "One flying machine—equivalent to seventy horses" (Holden, 1993). The plane was fast and could climb easily. Its one drawback was that it was difficult to control. The balance of the craft was essential to the safety of its occupants. If a passenger did not occupy the rear seat, a sandbag was required to offset the weight of the pilot seated in front. The gyroscope effect of the large Gnome engine with cylinders revolving around the drive shaft could also cause control issues.

In Mineola, a month before the Boston Air Meet, Harriet made three practice flights in her new plane and another early on the day of the event. During the second test flight she substituted a passenger for balance, rather than using the sand bag. A gentleman named Walter Bonner from Montana, who had traveled to Boston to see Harriet perform, was thrilled to be selected to participate in the trial run. It was not her intended goal, but by using Bonner to test her plane, Harriet also garnered another first—the first woman to fly a passenger in an aircraft. During her last practice maneuver, Harriet reverted to the sand bag for balance. She climbed to altitude but suddenly the machine shot upward, causing one wing to dip and the engine to stall. The plane began a rapid free fall, its nose to the earth. Somehow, Harriet was able to stabilize the plane before it struck the ground, and landed without further incident. She described the experience to her long-time mechanic Albert Houpert. He could not explain what happened and after a thorough inspection determined there was nothing wrong with the plane. He reminded Harriet that any airplane may lose balance in the air, especially if hit with an unexpected gust of wind. This conversation would haunt him later.

Two female journalists, Elizabeth Hiatt Gregory and Gertrude Stevenson, interviewed Harriet shortly before her Boston exhibition. Each came close to being Harriet's first female passenger. Stevenson even posed sitting in the back seat of the Bleriot, outfitted in flying togs similar to the ones Harriet wore. "You know," Harriet quipped, "this will make dandy cable news. You will be the first woman passenger to fly with a woman pilot—good enough to make headlines all over Europe" (*New York Times*, 1912).

This historic first for Harriet was not to be. As Stevenson reported in a story for the *Boston Herald* after Harriet's death, "That might have been me that day. It was only after I was safe at home that I came to grips with the reality of the horror—that the brave, clever, charming woman with whom I had laughed and joked scarcely one hour before had made her final flight. The machine, where I so gaily sat while pictures of Miss Quimby and myself were taken, had plunged into the muddy waters of Dorchester Bay" (*New York Times*, 1912).

A coin toss determined the lucky passenger to accompany Harriet in the early evening of July 1, 1912. William Willard, the enamored meet organizer, won the honor to fly with Harriet on the twenty-mile round-trip to Boston Light and back, to the envy of his sons, Charles and Harry.

While outwardly flamboyant, Harriet was always a cautious flyer. She checked her aircraft meticulously before every flight and worked closely with her mechanic to make sure all was in order before takeoff. At twilight, a smiling Harriet emerged from the hangar dressed in her plum jumpsuit. As she moved toward her plane, Harriet flashed her antique bracelet fashioned from the tusk of a wild boar and caressed the Ganesha clutched in her hand, as if to waken its positive spirit. She patiently responded to reporters' questions, giving particular attention to those concerning the technical parts of the Bleriot XI. When asked about a possible water landing if the engine should fail while flying over the harbor, Harriet calmly replied, "A water landing is alright in a Bleriot, unless you come down head first. Though if we come down 'pancake' the broad wings would float us for two hours or more." She paused for a moment and then, in what was almost an afterthought, joked, "But I am a cat—and I don't like cold water" (*New York Times*, 1912).

Harriet climbed into the cockpit, grandly tossed her cape to Stevens, and waved to the crowd. Houpert made a last-minute inspection of the warping mechanism beneath the fuselage, while Stevens exchanged some brief words with Willard. Everything was a go. Willard climbed into his seat behind Harriet. She gave the signal and Houpert pulled the propeller through one turn. Harriet flipped the switch and the propeller spun again, this time igniting the seven-cylinder engine. The mechanic exerted all his weight for a final spin of the propeller. The engine sputtered as each cylinder fired. The craft shook as the Bleriot's powerful engine lurched, thrusting the plane forward. It took four men to hold the machine by its horizontal stabilizer and landing gear as it strained at an invisible leash. Harriet lay on the throttle to increase gas flow to the engine. She tested the rudder pedals, then on Houpert's nod to proceed, tested the warping level and checked the wings.

Satisfied, Harriet waited another ten seconds to make sure the engine sound met her approval. She smiled her familiar smile and gave the thumbs-up. The ground crew released the plane and she moved into her takeoff roll.

Within seconds, the Bleriot ascended gracefully into the air and Harriet and her passenger began the twenty-seven-mile course around Boston Light. Right on schedule, twelve minutes into the flight, Harriet flew past Boston Light. At an altitude of 2,000 feet, she gently maneuvered the rudder and with a slight warp of the wings, came out of a descending turn around the lighthouse. The sun was setting and the sky had turned a brilliant orange. Five thousand spectators watched the silhouette of the dragonfly-like monoplane gliding across the blazing sky. Then suddenly, and for no apparent reason, some in the crowd noticed the plane's tail tilt abruptly skyward. It appeared, at least for a moment to those on the ground, that Harriet was not sure what to do. Spectators watched as she seemed to fight for control, presumably pulling back on the elevator stick to straighten the plane. For a moment, the craft seemed to respond to her command.

Harriet knew that the two-passenger Bleriot XI was known for balance problems. What she had not realized was that Willard had fallen from the plane. His body had ejected from the aircraft, folded in two like a swimmer catapulting from a diving board. Within seconds, the plane canted forward again like a bucking bronco in a rodeo. This time, as the plane went perpendicular, Harriet herself was ejected. As the plane somersaulted toward the earth, transfixed spectators stared in horror as it and the bodies of Harriet and her passenger soared downward, eerily side-by-side, headfirst into harbor waters 200 feet from shore. Only after the bodies had disappeared beneath the waves did the terrified crowd break from the stands.

Harry Willard rushed into the bay to reach his father but was restrained by onlookers. Several nearby boaters jumped into the sound to search for the victims. Reporting from the crash site, the *Boston Globe* said the bodies surfaced instantly, while the *New York Times* contradicted the report, noting that the two hit with such impact they were submerged in several feet of mud. Given the force with which both bodies would have slammed into the earth, especially at low tide into water less than four feet deep, the latter assessment seemed the more accurate. According to the *Globe*, it first appeared Harriet might still be alive and doctors at the scene worked for several minutes to revive her (*Boston Globe*, 1912).

The Massachusetts State Cavalry kept the hushed group of onlookers back while Harriet and Willard were transported to Quincy Hospital. Autopsies revealed that Harriet had died on impact and Willard had drowned. Eerily, the Bleriot monoplane flew itself out of the water and glided along the surface to a stop. Investigators determined that as the plane's wheels touched water, its landing gear was tripped and it somehow nosed over on its back, sustaining minimal damage. Examination of the plane's aneroid barometer indicated Harriet had reached an altitude of 5,000 feet. Eleven months after earning her pilot's license, Harriet Quimby was gone.

Aviator Earle Ovington, who witnessed the crash, reported that the plane had been stable and straight and that Harriet had demonstrated no signs of difficulty controlling the craft. He remarked at the grace with which the plane landed in the bay before "turning turtle" after ridding itself of its passengers. While inspecting the barely damaged plane, Ovington noticed that the left rudder wire controlling the steering had caught on the end of the vertical warping lever that operated the wings, leading him to speculate that the caught wire had caused the plane to veer left and pitch Willard from his seat. Albert Houpert disagreed. He insisted that the wires could have easily caught fire on the way down, or upon impact, perhaps fearing that he would be blamed for the tragedy. Those familiar with Bleriot aircraft, however, knew of its design flaws. In a letter to the editor in *Scientific American*, Ovington pointed out that the warping level in Harriet's latest Bleriot plane differed from other models he was familiar with including his own, reconfirming that he did not believe the crash resulted from mechanic error, but a flaw in the Bleriot design (*Leslie's Illustrated Weekly*, 1912).

Endless arguments followed about how the crash could have occurred. Pilot Lincoln Beachey, who within the year would also die in an aviation accident, surmised that Harriet, as a delicate female, could have been overcome by a sudden rush of wind and fainted, causing her to lose control of the plane. Curiously, some blamed the crash on the good-luck bracelet and Harriet's favorite talisman, the Ganesha, which had sunk deep in the mud close to Harriet's body. Retrieved and presented to her long-time *Leslie's* colleague John Sleicher, it sat on his desk for the remainder of his career. Several stories suggested Harriet had experienced momentary vertigo or that some type of gyroscopic force caused the plane to unexpectedly arc to the left. Aviator Glenn Curtiss argued that such an accident would never have occurred if Harriet and her passenger had been strapped in, although eyewitnesses that day claim they saw Harriet fasten an ankle restraint, a precursor to seat belts used today, that should have secured her. Initially, no one mentioned that Willard had appeared to lean sharply forward toward the cockpit, perhaps to speak to Harriet, and that perhaps she had removed the restraint to push him back into his seat. A large man, his weight might easily have offset the fragile balance of the Bleriot XI. Those who knew Harriet thought she was too safety and detail conscious to assume such risks. Nevertheless, at the time of the crash, neither Harriet nor William were strapped in.

Seat belts were not yet mandatory and were used by only a few European pilots. Nor were pilots displaying complex maneuvers such as "loop-the-loop" and "yank and bank" turns that evolved as more powerful and better-built aircraft came along. Just three weeks before her death, Harriet had written about the latest aviation safety improvements. A photo accompanying the piece showed a type of shoulder harness worn by some European aviators, but which had not yet caught on in the US. No one envisioned that this awkward-looking contraption would become the safety apparatus worn by travelers today.

A. Leo Stevens believed that Willard had, in fact, caused the accident when he suddenly bent forward to speak to Harriet. Stevens claimed to have warned Willard twice before the flight not to move around or leave his seat under any circumstances. According to Stevens, William was a man of some girth, weighing well over 200 pounds, and prone to sudden impulses. "Many times when talking with him I have known him to leap from his seat to tell me of an idea that suddenly came to him," he told reporters. "I believe that as they were coming back to the landing field, Willard was overcome with enthusiasm for Harriet's splendid performance. For a moment, he forgot the danger of moving about and stretched forward, or worse, stood up, to express his congratulations" (Holden, 1993).

Stevens theorized that this would upset the craft's delicate balance. To support his contention, Stevens pointed out that the hood on the machine that separated pilot from passenger had been removed to make Harriet's access easier, an unusual practice. Two boards were all that separated the two. Harriet would have had no way of seeing Willard lean toward her and would not have had time to take corrective action. The Boston Aeronautical Society agreed and announced that the official cause of the accident was the lack of fore and aft stability to counteract rotation on the plane's center of gravity.

An explanation of what likely happened also appeared in the August 1912 issue of *Aircraft* magazine. In "The Danger of the Lifting Tail and Its Probable Bearing on the Death of Miss Quimby," Walter H. Phipps reported that the Bleriot XI featured a horizontal tail wing that was meant to help offer longitudinal stability to the two-passenger plane. However, when the aircraft nosed down beyond a certain angle, the tail surface could provide unwanted lift that increased with plane speed until a critical moment was reached. At that point, the author explained, it would have been impossible to get the tail down even if the elevator stick was pulled back. The faster the machine dives, the more lift the tail provides until the plane is in a vertical position. This would cause the pilot and passenger to be hurled from the plane—unless they were strapped in. Phipps listed in his article a dozen or more pilots who died in Bleriot monoplanes under similar circumstances. With today's advances in aviation technology, this analysis still appears to be the most credible. No matter what the explanation—too steep a glide, a gust of wind, the broken rudder wire, or the lifting tail plane—the fact remains that the Bleriot was a fragile, problem-ridden, and unforgiving aircraft even for experienced flyers like Harriet. Like so many others, even she was a victim of aviation's age of innocence.

Spectators on the ground that early evening were not the only ones stricken with disbelief. Flyer Blanche Scott was airborne and witnessed the horrifying chain of events from her vantage point in the sky. She later told reporters that she was so shaken she had difficulty maintaining control of her own aircraft, a Martin biplane. The *New York Times* reported that Scott repeatedly tried to descend, but faltered with each attempt. After several minutes, she was able to turn the nose of her machine downward and landed abruptly, but safely. Scott explained that she had tried to land immediately when she saw her friend hit the ground, but the chaotic crowd stampeding toward the crash site made it impossible. She knew many could be literally sliced in two by her propeller so she was forced to wait, watching from above.

After Harriet's death, Scott became one of the few remaining women pilots in America. Asked by reporters if she would continue flying, she replied that Harriet's crash would not deter her. Like all flyers, Scott knew that it was only a matter of time before something would go wrong. "If aviators choose to stay in the game," said Scott, "the reality is we may die. We all know this and that's why all flyers are fatalists. We accept what will be, will be" (*World Magazine*, 1912).

The deaths of Harriet and Willard marked the forty-second and forty-third aviation fatalities recorded during the first six months of 1912. This was one distinction where Harriet did not rank first. She was the second American woman to die in an air accident. Pilot Julia Clark's death preceded Harriet's by just two weeks when her biplane clipped a grove of trees on takeoff. As the craft fell to earth, the motor mounted behind the pilot's seat broke loose and landed on top of her, crushing her.

Following Harriet's crash, officials called a halt to the day's program, but in true show-business tradition, assured the crowd that the event would continue the following afternoon. Only black crepe streamers attached to the flying wires of participating aircraft and black armbands worn by pilots reminded spectators of the previous day's tragedy. But attendance was sparse in the remaining days of the event and it ended more than $30,000 in the red.

Always dubious of women flyers, the Aero Club used the tragedy as an opportunity to suspend the licenses of seven male and female pilots for participating in what they called an unsanctioned event, and to call attention to safety issues. If aeronautics was to become a legitimate industry worldwide, it was time for aircraft builders to address these concerns, starting with the monoplane.

Harriet's death unleashed a storm of criticism from the aviation community and the public. An editorial in the *New York Sun* declared, "The sport is not one for which women are physically qualified. As a rule, they lack strength, presence of mind, and the courage to excel as aviators. It is essentially a man's sport and pastime. In the world's now long list of aviation fatalities, none has caused more profound grief than the tragic demise of Harriet Quimby" (*Smithsonian*, 1984).

The renowned British aviator Claude Grahame-White, whose record Harriet was attempting to break, responded to a question from a reporter for the *Detroit Free-Press* regarding "women who aviate." "Women are temperamentally unfit for flight because they are prone to panic," he said. "When calamity overtakes women pupils as eventually I fear it will, I shall feel in a way responsible for their sudden decease" (Holden, 1993). Grahame-White was known to be an opportunist and shameless self-promoter. He openly opposed women learning to fly but accepted women as students to support the high cost of maintaining his many airplanes. And he did not stand alone in his convictions.

John Moisant, protégé of Louis Bleriot and owner of Moisant School of Aviation. San Diego Air and Space Museum.

Poster announcing the Belmont Air Meet in October 1910, where Harriet's passion for aviation was born. National Air and Space Museum, Smithsonian Institute.

John Moisant flying his Bleriot monoplane at the Belmont Air Meet. John Carruthers Aviation Collection at Harvey Mudd College, California.

A. Leo Stevens, aeronaut, celebrated balloon builder, and friend of the Moisant brothers. He later became Harriet's manager and rumored lover and arranged for what turned out to be Harriet's final flight at the Boston Air Meet, July 1912. San Diego Air and Space Museum.

Poster advertising the Moisant Aviation School in Garden City, New York. The Wright Brothers would not accept female flight students at their school in North Carolina. Library of Congress.

Poster advertising the first air meet held on
Dominguez Field (near what is now the city of
Carson, south of Los Angeles). Harriet had covered
this inaugural event for *Leslie's Weekly*. California State
University Dominguez Hills Archives.

Harriet arrived for flight lessons before dawn each morning. Library of Congress.

Matilde Moisant (left) and Harriet pose for photographers at the October 1910 air meet. (Notice the sailor collar, which Harriet's later flying attire would copy.) Library of Congress.

Harriet all smiles after passing her pilot's exam with flying colors. Library of Congress.

Harriet points skyward, as if testing
for "still air." Library of Congress.

Harriet (right, center) and Matilde Moisant with flight instructor Alpert Houpert (kneeling between Matilde and Harriet) as they wait for the weather to clear before Harriet's pilot's exam. Library of Congress.

Harriet ready for take-off. Library of Congress.

Albert Houpert, Harriet's flight instructor. He later became a member of her flight crew. Library of Congress.

Reproduction of a letter from the Aero Club notifying Harriet that she had officially earned her pilot's license, becoming the first American woman to do so. Library of Congress.

AERO CLUB OF AMERICA
207 MADISON AVENUE
NEW YORK, NEW YORK

August 2d 1911

Miss Harriet Quimby, 225 Fifth Avenue, New York City

MADAM: We take pleasure in informing you that in a meeting of the Executive Committee held this afternoon, you were granted an aviation pilot's license of the Aero Club of America. This book is all made up and lacks only the signature of our acting president, which will be obtained tomorrow morning.

We find that the only other aviation pilot's license granted to a woman under the 1911 rules is that of Mme. Draincourt of France, who passed the tests in a Caudron biplane.

Should no mail advice (sic) to the contrary reach us within the next few days from Europe, you can accordingly consider yourself the only woman to have qualified under the new 1911 rules on a monoplane.

Regarding the landing made by you at the close of your first distance test on August 1st, we should say that accurate landing is not a record internationally recognized so that we do not know how this performance compares with the best made in Europe. We can state, however, that at this date, it is the most accurate landing made in America in a monoplane under official supervision.

The American record for accurate landings is 1 foot, 5 ½ inches by Mr. Sopwith on his biplane. We do not officially make any distinction between types of aeroplanes in this record; we cannot see, however, how there can be any objection to your landing being referred to as an "American record for monoplanes" at this date, as this is what it is in fact.

Yours sincerely,

C.F. Campbell-Wood (signed)
Secretary

Wilbur Wright with Mrs. Hart O. Berg, the wife of a Wright employee and the first woman to ride as a passenger in a Wright Brothers biplane. Women were not admitted to the Wright Aviation School in North Carolina. Library of Congress.

Elise Raymonde Deroche, aka the Baroness de La Roche of France, the first woman in the world to earn a pilot's license in 1910, just fifteen months before Harriet. Library of Congress.

A Ganesha, with its elephant head and human body, is worshipped as the Buddhist patron of good luck. Superstitious throughout her life, Harriet was known to carry her "lucky Ganesha" with her in the cockpit of her plane. Source unknown.

Harriet supported her parents throughout her life. William and Ursula join their daughter on a European vacation. Library of Congress.

Harriet was captivated by faces. Photos from one of Harriet's many stories filed from around the world. Many of her travel photographs for *Leslie's* were later compiled in a series of books published by the Leslie-Judge Company and entitled *Around the World with a Camera 1910–1919*. Reprinted from *Leslie's Weekly* for *Around the World with a Camera 1910–1919*.

Harriet always captured the expressions of her subjects. Reprinted from *Leslie's Weekly* for *Around the World with a Camera 1910-1919*.

Harriet called this spread "Strange Sights in the Heart of Erin's Isle." She was curious about world cultures. Reprinted from *Leslie's Weekly* in *Around the World with a Camera 1910-1919*.

Harriet's photos of "Curious Country Scenes Motoring in
Europe." Reprinted from *Leslie's Weekly for Around the World with
a Camera 1910-1919.*

Harriet told female supporters, "Flying is easier than voting." At the time Harriet earned her pilot's license, the right to vote for women was still nine years in the future. Library of Congress.

After receiving her license, Harriet earned money by participating in air meets around the country. Thousands would gather at aerodomes. Source unknown.

Harriet's mother, Ursula, was a suffragette who wanted more for her daughter than life as a farmer's wife, although Harriet adamantly claimed she was not a feminist. Library of Congress.

Alexander Kenealy, editor of the *London Daily Mirror*, at the time of Harriet's English Channel flight. He was responsible for the Ganesha publicity stunt in which Harriet cut the head from her Ganesha to promote the event. Harriet restored the head upon her return to the US. Three months later, she was gone. The "lucky" Ganesha was found buried in the mud beneath her body at the crash site. From the book *Publish and Be Damned!* by H. Cudlipp.

Chapter Five

LEGACY: A LIFE TOO SHORT (1875–1912)

"If you are afraid, of course, you will never succeed."
—Harriet Quimby

Shortly before her death, Harriet wrote an article for *Good Housekeeping entitled "Aviation as a Feminine Sport," in which she offered* her opinion of aviation as a career for women. The article appeared two months after her death in September 1912. Her enthusiasm is particularly poignant in light of her tragic death. She writes:

> There is no sport that affords the same amount of excitement and joy, or exacts in return so little muscular strength, as flying. It is easier than walking or driving; simpler than golf or tennis. There is no reason why the aeroplane should not open a fruitful occupation for women. I see no reason why they cannot realize handsome incomes by carrying passengers between adjacent towns, supervising parcel delivery, taking photographs, or conducting schools of flying. Any of these things it is now possible to do. The number of men fliers will always outnumber the women, just as chauffeurs outnumber the women who drive automobiles. But with the establishment of fuel supply and landing stations, there is no reason why we cannot have airlines for distances of 50 to 60 miles. This mode of travel would be delightful…

Harriet may have been alluding to the next step for women in flight—another first for her and another path-blazing opportunity for women. In June 1912, one month before her death, Harriet had received a US Post Office permit that would make her the first woman to transport mail by air. She was set to demonstrate the potential for airmail by flying from Boston to New York on July 7, in what was to be the grand finale to the now infamous Boston Light Air Meet. It would be another year before pilot Marjorie Stinson became the first woman to fly the mail.

Two weeks after her death, *Leslie's Weekly* published a touching tribute to its long-time employee:

A brilliant light in the literary firmament has been extinguished. The tragic death of Harriet Quimby, truly the most famous aviatrix, while flying with a passenger at the Boston Air Meet, put a sad and sudden end to a career that promised only great things for literature, art, and science.

Miss Quimby conducted the dramatic department of our publication with an independence and fairness that won general admiration, critical art reviews that were marvels of style and expression, while as a writer on aeronautics she was one with the highest caliber.

She took up aviation less than two years ago, first as a pastime, but afterward because she became a devoted advocate to the science itself. She firmly believed in aeronautics as crucial for the progress of the century, and gave her young life as sacrifice to a sense of duty.

The staff of *Leslie's*, with whom she had been a willing, helpful, faithful worker and associate for the past nine years, feel her loss as few others can. But we have the comfort of many assurances from her lips that, in her innermost soul, she felt no fear of death because she remained serene that in death she would open the door to fadeless immortality (*Leslie's Illustrated Weekly*, 1912).

For several months, Harriet's final articles continued to appear in *Leslie's*. Both colleagues and her hundreds of readers were moved by the scope of her talent and passion for so many social issues of the time. During her career she had covered a broad spectrum of topics in more than 250 articles, such as "Through the Opera Glass," "Helpful Household Hints," and "Can a Woman Run an Automobile?" not to mention her columns on social issues like immigration, child labor, and unfair working conditions.

One *Leslie's* colleague charged with the task of clearing her desk discovered an unfinished piece entitled "Lost in the Sky." In it, Harriet wrote:

Nobody likes to be lost. There is a wretchedness about it most pathetic. Our hearts go out to the lost child, we join in the search for the missing, whether we be neighbors or strangers. The instinct to go to the rescue is always the same.

It is a new experience to be lost in the sky, but it is as real and as trying as to be lost in the midst of earth's wilderness or on the infinite expanse of the waters of the sea. I speak with knowledge. Twice I have been lost while driving a monoplane.

The sense of loneliness and helplessness one feels while driving a thousand feet above the earth in a swiftly moving monoplane, with nothing but everlasting sky above and the horizon around with no signs of recognition from the distant earth below, is overwhelming and indescribable. One can do nothing but look and hope. One must drive on, amid the roar of the motor blade making its thousand revolutions a minute.

The aviator who is lost feels no helping hand reach out to him. He looks for none. There is nothing to do except keep an eye keenly on the watch for some friendly meadow or spread of water, indicating the location of the aviation field to which a safe descent can be made. But it is never hopeless, for the aviator knows that if darkness supervenes, it will, in all probability, disclose the beacon fires of watchers on the field. If one has not flown too far away, he can easily recognize, from his commanding place of vantage, the blazing pile where the watchers wait.

Why should I be lost in the air? It is the easiest thing in the world. The landmarks you see, as you walk or ride on the surface of the earth, are not recognized as such by the flyer. On the earth you see these things straight ahead or to the side, within the horizontal range of the eye. From a balloon or an aeroplane you see the roof, not the sides of the house; pinnacles that pierce the sky, not the majestic towers that command the vision from the side view.

Recall your own experience and your exclamation of surprise after you have gone to the top of the Washington Monument at the national capital, the Arch d'Triumphe in Paris, the top of Bunker Hill in Boston, or of a skyscraper in any city. You find yourself puzzled as to the points of the compass. The most familiar buildings, streets, and avenues are almost indistinguishable except as you study the vista spread before you.

Is it a wonder that one gets lost in the sky? Remember that from the dizzy height of a monoplane as one looks over the side of a car, the earth seems flattened out, rivers shrink until they become no larger than brooks, the hills are leveled and fields of variegated color appear like spaces on a checkerboard. The earth is flat, not round, as the aeroplanist sees it. But I could always pick my landing at any time when I was lost, for I kept sailing about until I found a suitable place. Then I came down and was happy (*Leslie's Illustrated Weekly*, 1912).

Before she traveled to Boston for what would be her last flight, Harriet had also penned a handwritten note to her parents in New York, similar in tone to the closing remarks of her unpublished piece. "If bad luck should befall me," she wrote, "I want you to know that I will meet my fate rejoicing" (*New York Times*, 1912).

A memorial service was held on July 4, 1912, at the funeral parlor of Frank E. Campbell in Manhattan, not far from where she had lived. The Reverend James Wasson read from the Book of Revelations. He told gatherers, "... But in our sorrow there rests still another joyful note, for we realize that through her death there has come progress and that, therefore, Harriet Quimby's life was a victory over those elements that brought on her very end. Through her, we reach nearer to the far off goal of hope. Her name now joins a long list of those who have freely given their lives so the world might be greater and grander" (*New York Times*, 1912).

Hundreds of people, including members of the Italian Aero Club, of which she was an honorary member; representatives from the Aeronautical Society of America, once so critical of her success; colleagues from *Leslie's Weekly*; prominent members of the theater community; government officials; and fellow flyers all gathered to pay their final respects. Harriet's mother gave each attendee a rose to place on the casket. She told guests that Harriet was laid to rest in the white dress she had planned to wear at a luncheon recognizing her achievements as an aviator later that week.

The following day, Harriet was buried at Woodland Cemetery on Staten Island. Perhaps it was just another of her many superstitions, but Harriet feared her body might be used for experimental purposes and requested that her remains be sealed in a copper-covered, burglar-proof vault. Nor, she had instructed, was her date of birth to appear on her headstone.

A year later, A. Leo Stevens moved her remains to a permanent burial site at Kenisco Cemetery at Valhalla, New York. He lived the remainder of his life in Cooperstown, New York, where he demonstrated the art of ballooning to youngsters. In 1944, he died in a car crash on his way to Washington, DC, where he was to file another one of his many patents, this one for a safety chute for pilots. For many years, he had sponsored an annual prize in his name to honor the inventor of a new product that would contribute to pilot safety. It was believed that he never got over Harriet's untimely end.

Five years after her death, Harriet's good friend Clara Bell Brown recalled their meeting in San Francisco many years before and how Harriet had proclaimed confidently, "Something tells me that I shall do something someday (Brown, 1997)." Brown told reporters she remembered looking at Harriet, thinking that this radiant and beautiful spirit could pass through the crime-ridden and grimy streets of Chinatown or into the grandest ballroom in San Francisco, and her very presence would remain goddess-like and unfazed.

Editors at the *San Francisco Call*, where Harriet began her writing career, remembered her passing with a poem dedicated to her memory:

Rare girl of pencraft, on Bleriot's wings,
Serene and smiling, lady unafraid
you soared above the groundlings of your trade,
braving that fate which fate remorseless flings.
But you with vision, courage, flew afar;
your mentor was the strong-willed Albatross.

America lost a powerful advocate for aviation. She strongly believed that the United States was falling behind other nations such as England and France in the development of aviation technology, pilot safety policies, and commercial, as well as humanitarian, applications. There is no doubt that her accomplishments led the way for future female pilots such as Amelia Earhart, who often spoke of Harriet as her inspiration and personal hero. "To cross the English Channel in 1912 required more bravery and skill than to cross the Atlantic today," Earhart said. "We must remember to always pay respect to America's first great woman flier's accomplishments (Earhart, 1932).

Earhart liked to point out the similarities between herself and her hero. Harriet was born in Michigan, Amelia in Kansas. Amelia's grandparents and Harriet's parents were both pioneers and early settlers in their respective regions of the country. Both of their mothers came from a higher social status than their fathers. Harriet had nine siblings, but only she and her sister Kitty survived childhood. Amelia, too, had one sibling that survived childhood. However, Harriet's sister left home at age fourteen and was never heard from again, while Amelia and her sister remained close even though Amelia's unconventional lifestyle did not suit her sister. As adults, both Harriet and Amelia would move in elite social circles. Harriet socialized with luminaries such as Jack London, D. W. Griffith, and Louis Bleriot; Amelia was friends with Will Rogers, Mae West, and Charles Lindbergh. Though the ladies' lives would come to an end doing what they loved best, unfortunately for us all, they left all too soon.

In the 100-plus years since her death, Harriet's recognition has primarily focused on her contribution to aviation. But there was so much more she left for us to ponder, so many firsts to challenge and inspire us. Perhaps her greatest contribution was to remind us that we should live life to the fullest and remain true to ourselves. Male or female, all who met her admired her intelligence, independence, beauty, compassion for the human condition, and desire to bring about results. As she always said, "If you are afraid, of course, you shall never succeed" (*Leslie's Illustrated Weekly*, 1912). It's as timely a message today as it was in 1912.

Chapter Six

IN HER OWN WORDS

"To Americans living in the large cities, the danger of over-artificiality, of utter divorcement from nature, is most great and it is wonderful how a few plants on the roof, in the window, or the back yard, will take one back to the days when life was very sweet and the hours long" (*Leslie's Illustrated Weekly*, 1910).

"When Eve plucked the fig leaf in the Garden of Eden and converted it into a costume, there began a tragedy which has ever since been attached to the problem of clothes . . . but a pretty woman is pretty whatever her dresses may be" (*Leslie's Illustrated Weekly*, 1910).

"No country in the world is more adaptable to romance; no more literary or dramatic, than is California with its tropical jungles of flowers, its rose trees, which from a single trunk grows and spread over an entire patio . . . so saturated with romance is the very air which floats in from the Pacific . . . extending from one side of California to the other" (*San Francisco Call*, 1901).

The production of *The Foolish Virgin* fell as flat as an overdone omelet soufflé. The same may be said of the acting of Mrs. Campbell, who, in my opinion, has been highly overrated" (*Leslie's Illustrated Weekly*, 1906).

"Poetical China! Surely in many respects she scores over the more practical nations" (*Leslie's Illustrated Weekly*, 1910).

"Motoring is all right, but after seeing monoplanes in the air, I couldn't resist the desire to try the air lanes, where there are neither speed laws, nor traffic policemen, and where one needn't go all the way around Central Park to get across Times Square" (*Leslie's Illustrated Weekly*, 1910).

"The tires are too heavy for a woman to adjust, but almost any woman may tinker about the machinery and accomplish about the same results as a chauffeur of the opposite sex does. If she will only lose that dread of getting her hands all greasy and grimy" (*Leslie's Illustrated Weekly*, 1906).

"Functional but feminine" (*Leslie's Illustrated Weekly*, 1911)!

"I just wanted to be first, that's all" (*Leslie's Illustrated Weekly*, 1911).

Harriet brought her own style to flight attire, which set the standard for female aviators after her. Her stunning plum outfits could easily adapt to a walking skirt. Library of Congress.

A radiant Harriet was never happier than before taking to the air. (Note the slightly chipped front tooth—only noticeable in photographs and allegedly her only beauty flaw.) Library of Congress.

Blanche Stuart Scott, who flew during Harriet's time but never earned her license, continued to wear thick sweaters, trouserettes, and bulky boots and hats. Library of Congress.

Harriet looks at the spot where Louis Bleriot landed after his successful channel crossing in 1909. She flew the route followed by her mentor John Moisant, from England to France to avoid the daunting cliffs of Dover. Library of Congress.

Louis Bleriot, the Frenchman who invented the first working monoplane adopted by his protégé John Moisant and Harriet Quimby. Bleriot flew the English Channel in 1909. Library of Congress.

Harriet prepares for takeoff in her borrowed Bleriot at the Dover Aerodome on April 16, 1912. Library of Congress.

Rare photo of Harriet not wearing a hat, ca. 1912. *L'Aerophile*, April 1912.

Harriet approves the plane for takeoff. Library of Congress.

Gustav Hamel helps to secure Harriet to her seat before her
English Channel flight. Hamel had given her a compass to
help navigate the open waters. Library of Congress.

Harriet's ground crew holds back the Bleriot as Harriet
listens to the engine's hum. Library of Congress.

Harriet takes flight.

Villagers watch from shore as Harriet begins her descent after successfully crossing the English Channel.

Successful landing in Calais.

Harriet is greeted at Calais, France, following her record-breaking flight across the English Channel. Library of Congress.

The *New York Herald*'s reporting of the *Titanic*'s
tragic sinking twenty-four hours before Harriet's
English Channel record. The shocking news
relegated her achievement to the back pages of world
newspapers. *New York Herald* Archives.

The *New York American* headlines of the Titanic tragedy. *New York American* Archives.

The crowds in Calais cheering Harriet after her landing had no idea that the *Titanic* had sunk a few hours earlier. Library of Congress.

Even the *Daily Mirror*, which sponsored Harriet's
flight, did not report her accomplishment until
days later, and then buried the story in its back
pages. *Daily Mirror* Archives.

Famous Vin Fiz poster featuring Harriet, making her
the first female brand spokesperson for a major
advertising campaign. National Air and Space Museum.

Boston Light, Squantum, Massachusetts, the site of
Harriet's last flight on July 1, 1912. Source unknown.

Harriet routinely inspected her monoplane herself before every flight. Library of Congress.

Test flights were part of her routine to be sure all was in working order. Library of Congress.

Boston Light Air Meet organizer William Willard won the toss to accompany Harriet on her flight. San Diego Air and Space Museum.

Harriet strikes a confident pose with her new seventy-horsepower Bleriot XI before the Boston Light Air Meet on July 1, 1912. Smithsonian Institute.

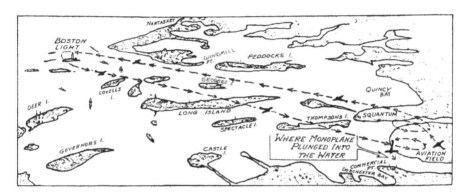

A *Boston Globe* artist drawing traces Harriet's flight path at Boston Light. Smithsonian Institute.

Harriet Quimby lifts off at Boston Light Air Meet, July 1, 1912.

Harriet's death certificate. National Air and Space Museum.

Frank E. Campbell Funeral Parlor on Manhattan's upper East
Side in the early twentieth century. Still in operation today, it has
been the site for hundreds of notable memorial services,
including that of Rudolph Valentino. Source unknown.

Harriet's final
resting place in
Kensico Cemetery,
Valhalla, New York.
Author's collection.

Cover of *Good Housekeeping* published two months after
Harriet's death in which her article "American Bird
Women" appeared. National Air and Space Museum.

Amelia Earhart lauded Harriet as an inspiration to her and all female aviators who followed in her footsteps. The US Postal Service recognized Harriet in 1991 with a postage stamp issued in her honor. Copyright USPS. Reproduced with permission of US Postal Service.

Harriet Quimby, flying fair lady, in one of her favorite sailor-collar dresses. Library of Congress.

"I shall go to my fate rejoicing," Harriet wrote to
her parents before the Boston Light Air Meet.
Library of Congress.

Alan Cagan, who introduced the author to the
legacy of Harriet Quimby, stands in front of the
Cradle of Aviation Museum in Garden City, New
York. Author's collection.

BIBLIOGRAPHY

Bombardier, Marcella, "In the Sky, No Limits for Famed Aviatrix." *Boston Globe*, July 1912.

Brown, Robert. *Ganesh: Studies of an Asian God.* Albany: State University of New York Press, 1991.

Brown, Sterling. *First Lady of the Air: The Harriet Quimby Story.* Greensboro: Tudor Publishers, 1997.

Chaikin, Andrew. *Air and Space: The National Air and Space Museum Story of Flight.* New York: Bulfinch Press/Little Brown and Company, 1997.

De Lear, Frank. "What Killed Harriet Quimby?" *Yankee Magazine*, September 1979.

Earhart, Amelia. *The Fun of It.* New York: Harcourt Brace, 1932.

Jones, Terry Gwynn. "For a Brief Moment the World Seemed Wild About Harriet." *Smithsonian*, January 1984.

Harris, Sherwood. *The First to Fly: Aviation's Pioneer Days.* New York: Simon and Schuster, 1970.

Henderson, Robert M. *D. W. Griffith, The Years at Biograph.* New York: Straus and Giroux, 1970.

Heppenheimer, T. A. *Flight: A Photographic History of Aviation.* London: Carlton Books, 2003.

Holden, Henry M. *Her Mentor Was an Albatross.* New Jersey: Black Hawk Publishing Company, 1993.

Hopkins, J. "King of Aviators," *Air Force Magazine*, 1960.

Mitchell, Charles R., and Kirk House W. *Flying High: Pioneer Women in American Aviation.* Charleston: Arcadia Publishing, 2002.

Moisant, M. "Matilde Moisant: Early Bird Aviator," *AERO Magazine*, 1912.

Oakes, C. M., "Women in Aviation Through World War I," *Smithsonian*, 1978.

Ovington, Earle. "Not Miss Quimby's Fault." *Leslie's Weekly Illustrated*, August 1, 1912.

Patterson, K. *Influence: The Power to Change Anything.* New York: McGraw-Hill, 2007.

Philips, N. *Working Girls: An Illustrated History of the Oldest Profession.* London: Bloomsbury, 1991.

Phipps, Walter H. "The Danger of the Lifting Tail and the Probable Bearing on the Death of Harriet Quimby." *Aircraft*, August 1912.

Powell, Hugh. "Harriet Quimby: America's First Woman Pilot." *American Aviation Historical Society Journal*, Winter 1982.

Quimby, Harriet. "Curious Chinese Customs." *Leslie's Illustrated Weekly*, January 22, 1903.

___ "The Chorus Lady," *San Francisco Call*, 1906.

___ "A Woman's Exciting Ride in A Motor Car." *Leslie's Illustrated Weekly*, October 4, 1906.

___ "A Japanese Aeronaut to Startle the World." *Leslie's Illustrated Weekly*, August 5, 1909.

___ "How A Woman Learns to Fly (Part I)." *Leslie's Illustrated Weekly*, May 25, 1911.

___"How Can We Save Our Birds." *Leslie's Illustrated Weekly*, June 8, 1911.

___"Exploring the Airlanes." *Leslie's Illustrated Weekly*, June 22, 1911.

___"How A Woman Learns to Fly (Part II)." *Leslie's Illustrated Weekly*, August 17, 1911.

___"How I Won My Aviator's License." *Leslie's Illustrated Weekly*, August 24, 1911.

___"The Dangers of Flying and How to Avoid Them." *Leslie's Illustrated Weekly*, August 31, 1911.

___"An American Girl's Daring Exploit." *Leslie's Illustrated Weekly*, May 16, 1912.

___"New Things in the Aviation World." *Leslie's Illustrated Weekly*, June 6, 1912.

___"American Bird Women." *Good Housekeeping*, June 1912.

___"How I Made My First Big Flight Abroad." *FLY Magazine*, June 1912.

___"We Girls Who Fly and What We're Afraid Of." *The World Magazine*, July 14, 1912.

___"Aviation As A Feminine Sport." *Good Housekeeping*, September 1912.

___"Lost in the Sky." *Leslie's Illustrated Weekly*, November 28, 1912.

Stein, E. P. "Vin Fiz Reborn." *Airport Journal*, August 2011. "Woman in Trousers Daring Aviator." *The New York Times*, May 11, 1911, 6.

"Miss Quimby Wins Air Pilot License." *The New York Times*, August 2, 1911, 7.

"Quimby Flies the English Channel." *The New York Times*, April 17, 1912, 15.

"Woman to Fly With Mail: Miss Quimby Will Fly from Boston to New York." *The New York Times*, June 21, 1912, 14.

"Miss Quimby Dies in Airship Fall." *The New York Times*, July 2, 1912, 1.

"Quimby Tragedy Unexplained." *The New York Times*, July 3, 1912, 7.

"Services for Miss Harriet Quimby Tonight." *The New York Times*, July 4, 1912, 7.

"When Aviation Becomes Not Only Dangerous But Foolhardy." *The New York Times Magazine*, July 7, 1912.

INDEX